CREATIVE
QUILTMAKING
IN THE
MANDALA
TRADITION

CREATIVE QUILTMAKING IN THE MANDALA TRADITION

DESIGN AND PATTERN DEVELOPMENT

JEAN EITEL

CHILTON BOOK COMPANY

Radnor, Pennsylvania

Designed by Adrianne Onderdonk Dudden
Manufactured in the United States of America

Library of Congress Cataloging in Publication Data
Eitel, Jean.
    Creative quiltmaking in the mandala tradition.
    (Chilton needlework series)
    Bibliography: p. 171
    Includes index.
        1. Quilting—Patterns.   2. Mandala.   I. Title.
II. Series.
TT835.E46   1985   746.9'7   84-45696
ISBN 0-8019-7614-6

1 2 3 4 5 6 7 8 9 0   4 3 2 1 0 9 8 7 6 5

CONTENTS

DESIGNING MANDALA QUILTS–29

CREATIVE QUILTMAKING–41

FROM ORDINARY TO EXTRAORDINARY–55

AN INDIVIDUAL APPROACH TO QUILTMAKING–63

QUILTING STITCHES: THE FINISHING TOUCH–67

vii

CONTENTS

PREFACE

For the past several years I have been compulsively involved with the craft of quilt-making. This has occurred as the result of a background in fine arts coupled with a lifetime involvement with stitching. Quiltmaking brings me great joy and a sense of anticipation. Writing has become a way to share my philosophy of quilting in an effort to inspire and encourage other quiltmakers who want to design original quilts. I have discovered that the artistic journey involved in working out the design, color, symbolism, and textural components of each new quilt is as important as the finished product. The quiltmaking journey can be a growing experience that provides opportunities to explore new ideas and techniques.

Bouquets of thanks should be sent to the many stitchers and friends who have helped me by sharing their quilts and encouraging me to share the ideas and patterns that are included in this book.

I would particularly like to thank my first quilting teacher, Helen Van Epp, whose dedication to teaching the traditional methods of quiltmaking initially inspired me to turn all of my creative efforts to this craft.

Two of my daughters, Ellen and Heidi, helped me with many of the illustrations in this book, and my oldest daughter, Elaine, kept the house so that I could work. To them I give special thanks and love.

My husband, Fred, has showed limitless patience and support as the writing of this book has progressed, and I truly appreciate him for this.

The research and design of the many mandalas in this book could not have been done without the help of my sister, Janet Wright, who shared so many of her books with me.

A special friend, Katharine Ward, helped by proofreading the text and giving many helpful suggestions.

Much of the initial photography was done by my friend Alysoun Powell, and I thank her for her help. I also wish to thank Aloyse Yorko and Cathy Laessig, who encouraged me to take many of the photographs myself and who were unselfish in giving advice and support.

CREATIVE QUILTMAKING IN THE MANDALA TRADITION

IMAGES

A quilt, made of fabric and thread, is something much more than a warm bed covering. A quilt is symbolic of the care and love the maker put into the design and the selection of patterns and colors that were so painstakingly stitched together. Women throughout history have traditionally created visual images and symbols with fabric and thread that express the events and circumstances of their daily lives. Our ancestors, who stitched what we call masterpiece quilts, created them out of a basic human need to add some beauty to a life that was a struggle for survival in a new and unfamiliar land. The quilts themselves provided warmth against the harsh winter cold and were a necessary part of that struggle for survival. Quiltmaking and other needlearts gave women perhaps their only opportunity to make a statement about their environment and to add a touch of beauty to their homes, and the patterns and symbols they chose for their quilts expressed the joys and sorrows that made up the fabric of their lives.

Women in colonial America developed a creative folk art that was truly their own. The fabrics available to our founding mothers were limited in color and print, as well as in quantity. The only tools available to the first quilters were common household items, such as pencils, chalk, string, teacups, plates, spools, and a ruler. These limited resources did not stifle their creativity or their desire to give their best efforts to their craft. Instead, they used their ingenuity and, from their limited fabric palettes, selected patterns and colors that have become timeless in their beauty. Today, their imaginative approach to their work and their innnovative designs are admired and respected by art historians, museum curators, and collectors of folk art throughout the country. American methods of piecing, appliqué, and quilting are now taught around the world, and a sense of global community is shared by women everywhere who are currently exploring this art form.

Fig. 1–1 "Rose of Sharon" quilt designed in a
traditional mandala format, late nineteenth century.

Fig. 1–2 "Feathered Star" quilt in a geometric
mandala design, late nineteenth century.

Two words—*quilt* and *mandala*—describe the efforts of these early quiltmakers. Both words have ancient origins that bring to mind a variety of images and feelings. The word *quilt* is from the Old French *cuilte*, which means a sack with stuffing, a mattress, or a cushion. The dictionary defines a quilt as a coverlet for a bed made of two layers of fabric with a soft stuffing between and stitched in patterns through all thicknesses. *Quilt* is also a verb—the process of stitching together two pieces of cloth and a soft interlining.

Mandala is from the ancient Sanskrit, meaning circle, and is a Hindu or Buddhist symbol of the universe. In Jungian psychology the mandala represents the unity of the self. When used in this context, the mandala signifies more than just a circle in that it takes on a hidden and mystical meaning. Sometimes the mandala, or *magic circle*, is defined as a schematic representation of geometric shapes. A single simple shape such as the hexagon can be arranged in a formal scheme to create a mandala quilt. Mary

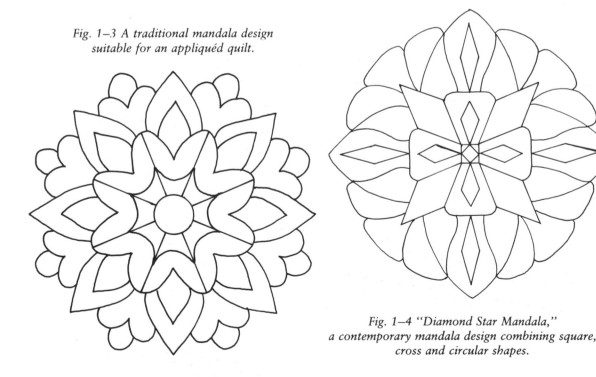

Fig. 1–3 *A traditional mandala design suitable for an appliquéd quilt.*

Fig. 1–4 *"Diamond Star Mandala," a contemporary mandala design combining square, cross and circular shapes.*

Anne Johnson used the hexagon, which quilters usually find in the familiar "Grand-mother's Flower Garden" arrangement, in a new and exciting arrangement for her mandala quilt, *Grandmother's Mosaic* (see color section, Figure 1).

The mandala symbol is used in a vast number of both antique and comtemporary quilts. Mandala brings to mind words such as *cosmos, universe, centering, mystical, mystery, medallion,* or *magic circle.* Even though they may be unaware of the different meanings of the word, many quilt artists instinctively choose to work with the mandala design. A simple design format for the mandala is a circle, a cross, or a square within a square.

The magic circle can incorporate many themes from daily life. We need only to become careful observers of our surroundings to find a theme for a magic circle quilt. A mandala can ripple gently from a center point as though a pebble had been thrown into a pond, or it can glide outward with the grace of a ballet or the fluid movements

Fig. 1–5 "Fractured Kaleidoscope,"
star mandala quilt block.

Fig. 1–6 *"Double Hearts" quilt, a typical wedding quilt, late nineteenth century.*

Fig. 1–7 *"Oak Leaf" quilt, late nineteenth century. Each block is a simple mandala design.*

of a folk dance. A mandala can march forth in fractured color as the tinted glass moves in a kaleidoscope, or it can burst upon you with a sudden display of brilliant color like a Fourth of July fireworks celebration.

Since all art forms are interrelated, it is not surprising that images from the performing arts, such as music or dance, are frequently used in quiltmaking. See, for example, the quilt entitled *Dancing Tulips* (see color section, Figure 2). The tulips in

Fig. 1–8 A "Princess Feather" quilt with swag border,
mid-nineteenth century.

the center of the quilt appear to be holding hands and dancing in a circle, which calls to mind images of folk dances. *Bravissimo* (see color section, Figure 3), a quilt made by Deanna Powell of Melbourne, Florida, was created for the Brevard Symphony and is based on the "kaleidoscope" pattern. This pattern can be put together in many ways by using dark, medium, and light values to create a variety of mandala designs. Music was the inspiration for this quilt, and musical images are quilted into the border areas.

One of the major goals—and challenges—of today's quiltmakers is to master and perfect the techniques of the craft of their ancestors. When each piece is finished, we stitch our names on the back of our work to record our identity, following the example of stitchers from the past. Only time will prove the lasting quality of our efforts. But by carefully selecting the images and symbols we use in our quilts, and by making them with great care, we will become part of a tradition of masterpiece quiltmakers, leaving a priceless legacy for future generations as we seek to ensure a continuity with the past. In a way, in fact, we ourselves as quilt artists will be part of a magic circle.

SYMBOLS: A SIGN LANGUAGE FOR QUILTMAKERS

Generations of imaginative quilters have incorporated symbols in their quilts that reflect their culture and the era in which they lived. They have established a tradition of creating symbols that convey messages which are *commonly accepted and understood* by quiltmakers everywhere. Today's innovative quiltmakers may choose to design symbols of their own to record an important event in their life or to express an idea. Whether they select traditional symbols or develop new ones, contemporary quilt artists give expression to their lives and experiences through the symbols they choose to stitch into their quilts.

A symbol is a sign, and yet, for it to have significance, it must be more than a sign. A sign simply points the way or gives direction, whereas a symbol stands for something more. A symbol should contain a life-meaning or truth. For a visual symbol to be more than a sign, it must convey a generally accepted idea or belief to the members of a particular community or culture.

Letters of the alphabet arranged into words are symbols of our language. If we think of language as symbols, then the symbols used by quilters become the sign language of the craft. When using symbols in a quilt, the quiltmaker should learn to look beyond the visual images for the message they express.

Symbolism has played a significant role in the visual arts throughout history. From the earliest civilizations, systems of symbols have been used as teaching tools and as an aid in remembering oral instruction. For centuries, the oral tradition was the only way people could record and remember their history and the events that gave meaning to their lives.

Some frequently used symbols in quilting are the pineapple, a symbol for hospitality, and the heart and hand, a symbol for friendship. Flowers, animals, and birds were also favorite symbols used by our quilting ancestors. A careful study will reveal the meanings of the symbols that quiltmakers used in the past. Among them were garlands of flowers, expressing the commitment of love; laurel wreaths for victory, eternity, or good fortune; the eagle for courage; the acorn for long life; and the oak branch for victory.

Flowers, in particular, had a unique symbolism of their own. A daisy was the symbol of innocence, red tulips represented a declaration of love, and a yellow tulip represented hopeless love. The rose also carried many messages of love. A red rose symbolized true love, and the red and white rose together showed unity. Jealousy was represented by a yellow rose and grace by a pink rose. A white rose meant "I am unworthy of you," and a ring of roses expressed eternal love.

The meaningful use of symbols should encourage us to look for the deeper or hidden message in a quilt. Symbolism is a pictorial language that gives expression to

Fig. 2–1 The Pineapple, symbol of hospitality.

Fig. 2–2 Traditional pineapple for quilters.

individual experiences. Symbols are one way of bringing important events of daily life into focus, and learning their meanings will enable us to select symbols for our quilts that will give future generations information about ourselves and our environment. The process of making a quilt should fill an emotional or creative need for the individual quiltmaker and also speak to others when the completed work is shared with family and friends or displayed in an exhibit.

Circle of Friends (see color section, Figure 4), a quilt made by Julie Goodman of Fayetteville, Arkansas, was intended to symbolize and remember the friendships she had found important to her in her quilting group in Florida, before she and her family moved away. If you meet regularly with a group of quilters in a guild or quilting bee,

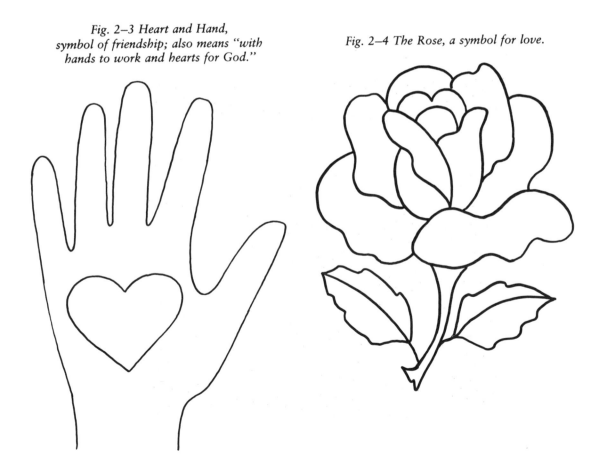

Fig. 2–3 Heart and Hand, symbol of friendship; also means "with hands to work and hearts for God."

Fig. 2–4 The Rose, a symbol for love.

you may have discovered that you come to have a better understanding of others by studying the symbols they choose for their quilts. If your group makes friendship quilts, a stimulating group project would be to research common quilting symbols and share at your meetings what you learn.

You might want to begin with a quilt that includes patriotic symbols. An eagle holding an olive or oak branch in one claw and arrows in the other is a symbol that represents the United States. Stars used on patriotic quilts represent divine guidance. Other patriotic symbols are the dove and olive branch for peace and the torch, which symbolizes truths that were borne by generations past and are to be given to generations of the future. Putting these symbols in a circular format to make a mandala design can be interpreted as an expression of unity of your quilting group.

The family is also a rich source for symbols. Symbols of warmth and caring can express family unity and love. Quilts can tell a story of family customs or record important family events. Displaying quilts on a bed, a table, or a wall can create a setting that will communicate a special spirit of caring and love to everyone who enters our homes. A family member's profession, community responsibilities, or cherished

Fig. 2–5 The Eagle, symbol of patriotism.

Fig. 2–6 The Dove, symbol of peace.

events, such as a graduation, marriage, or the birth of a baby, might suggest either the creation of a new symbol or the use of a traditional one in a quilt made for a special occasion.

Among the traditional symbols that are used to tell of family events are the Tree of Life, to record family history, the circle for enduring love, or the simple red square that appears in the center of a log cabin quilt block, representing the warmth of the hearth. Years ago, a sheaf of wheat tied with a ribbon was placed on the wedding table to wish the bride and groom a life of abundance and love. The pine cone symbolizes a fruitful life, and the cornucopia is a symbol of plenty associated with a good harvest and the family Thanksgiving holiday.

As contemporary quiltmakers and quilt artists, we actively participate in the quilting tradition by keeping alive symbols and patterns from the past. Through a better understanding of symbols, each quiltmaker has the opportunity to experiment with new

Fig. 2–7 Sheaf of Wheat, symbol of good fortune for the bride and groom.

Fig. 2–8 A mandala designed by the author for the Social Concerns Committee, Episcopal Diocese of Southeast Florida.

ideas and visual images to tell something of our lives, our family customs, and our secret hopes and dreams. Our finished quilts should speak for themselves through pattern, form, color, texture, and symbolism to create a unified whole. Perhaps future generations will study the quilts of today and marvel at the patience and ingenuity employed so painstakingly in an effort to preserve a fragment of our lives through the medium of needle and thread.

Through quiltmaking, we can gain the courage to share something uniquely our own with others. As we expand our knowledge of symbols and incorporate them in our quilts, we will come to know ourselves and our environment better. Learning more about oneself or one's environment through quiltmaking is only one of the rewards of the craft.

Fig. 2–9 Eagle and Star, *quilted wall hanging.*

COLOR HARMONIES

Writing a book about quilting—and particularly a book that deals with the use of symbolism in quilts—without talking about color would be an impossible task. The color choices a quiltmaker makes when she selects the fabrics for a quilt are very important, for color has a unique symbolic, as well as psychological, aspect. Many quilters often struggle with color combinations for their quilts long after they have decided upon the pattern and design.

Actually, we all know more about color than we realize. From the first time we opened our eyes as infants, we began to learn about color. A good observer will always be aware of color and in search of new combinations of color in her surroundings. The world of nature provides a vast array of exciting and unusual color combinations from which to select.

Colors can be divided into different groups that make them easier to understand and work with. One popular method is to group colors according to the four seasons. Colors could just as easily be grouped according to emotions, such as love, hate, contentment, or joy, or according to the four primal elements—earth, wind, fire, and water.

Painters classify colors in terms of tints, tones, hues, and shades. A *hue* is the brightest and purest form of a color and is the base for tints, tones, and shades. A *tint* is a color that has been mixed with white to create an effect of luminosity. A tint emphasizes a source of light, such as an area of bright sunlight in a room or a garden. A *tone* is a color that is mixed with gray and used to create an iridescent, pearl-like effect. A *shade* is a color that is mixed with black to create a lustrous or metallic image. The Amish use this color-classification technique to create the striking combinations in their quilts. Hues are associated with summer, shades with fall, tones with winter, and tints with spring.

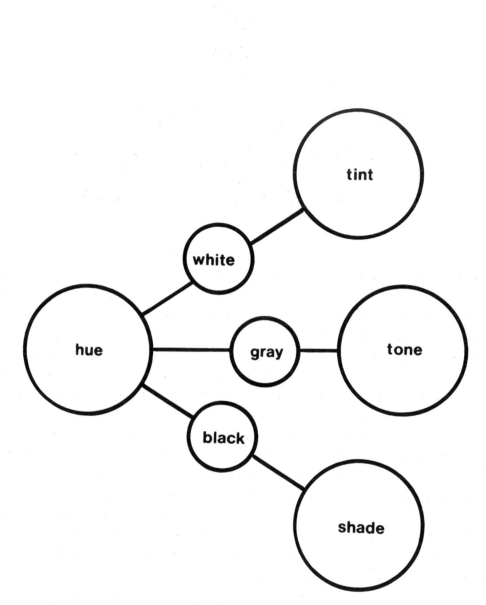

Fig. 3–1 Color Triangle. Adapted from Faber Birren, The Textile Colorist.

Artists also think of colors in terms of hue, value, and intensity. *Hue* is simply the name of the color itself, such as blue, red, yellow, or purple; hue also refers to the various color families. *Value* is the lightness or darkness of a color. The value of a color changes according to the amount of light it reflects. For example, colors in a room or in nature change in value as light increases or decreases throughout the day. Intensity is the brightness or dullness of a color, and it describes a color as either strong or weak, warm or cool. Red and yellow are warm colors, whereas blue and green are cool colors.

In *Concerning the Spiritual in Art*, the artist Wassily Kandinsky speaks of color as a musical symphony. He describes light blue as the flute, darker blue as a cello, and a deep navy as the sounds of an organ. Green is represented by the peaceful notes of a violin. Warm red can give a feeling of strength and determination and is heard as the strong ringing sounds of a trumpet. Purple is an English horn or the deep resonant tones of the wood instruments, such as the bassoon. Black represents silence.

Using a basic geometric shape, the triangle, Julie Goodman created the quilt entitled *Black* (see color section, Figure 5) which has a strong image of a cross in the center, with geometric forms and bold colors framing it. This quilt makes handsome use of a color that most quilters avoid.

–USING THE COLOR WHEEL–

Color is an important influence in our lives. We all have favorite colors and colors that we find unappealing and tend to avoid. Faber Birren, a color researcher who has devoted his life to the study of color and its effects on our psychological and emotional nature, has written many books on the subject including *The Textile Colorist*, which is a good sourcebook for quiltmakers. His color wheel and color triangle (Figures 3–1 and 3–2) are the mainstays of color theory in art. Our response to certain colors, and whether or not we like or dislike them, can reveal something about our personalities and emotions. A responsive, happy person usually reacts positively to color. A person who is inhibited may shy away from bright colors. A person who is indifferent to his emotional needs may seem to be unaffected by color.

Most of us learned the basics of the color wheel in elementary school. Understanding the color wheel and the positions of colors in relation to one another is essential for developing a greater understanding of using color in quilts. The three basic, or primary, colors are red, yellow, and blue, and they are indicated on the color wheel by the solid round symbols. Primary colors are pure colors because they contain no other color. Yellow, for example, has no red or blue in it.

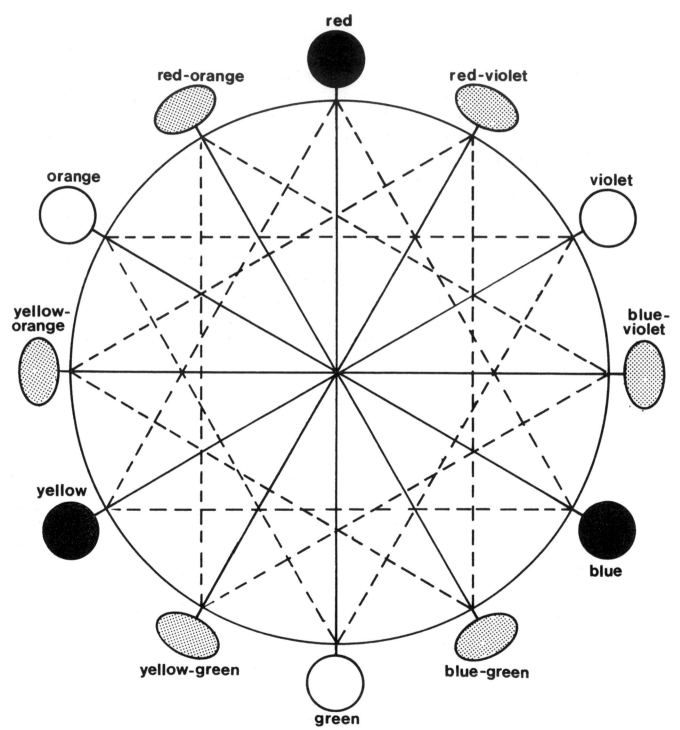

Fig. 3–2 *Basic color wheel with primary, secondary, and tertiary colors.*
Adapted from Faber Birren, The Textile Colorist.

red

red-orange

red-violet

orange

violet

yellow-orange

blue-violet

yellow

blue

yellow-green

blue-green

green

All other colors are created by combining differing amounts of the three primary colors. The mixed colors are also divided into groups. The secondary colors are created from equal amounts of red/blue, yellow/blue, and yellow/red to make violet, green, and orange. The secondary colors are represented on the color wheel by the open, round symbols. The tertiary colors made by combining a secondary color with one of the adjacent primary colors. There are six tertiary colors, indicated on the color wheel by ovals. By using the basic color wheel, it is easy to see how colors can be mixed with adjacent colors to make an infinite number of combinations.

Colors can also be mixed with their opposites on the color wheel. This usually produces browns of varying shades, depending on which set of opposites is used. Equal mixes of the primary or secondary colors will also produce a variety of browns or grays.

In selecting a color scheme for your quilts, you can use the color wheel to combine your fabrics in an aesthetic arrangement. There are three basic ways to do this. First, you can make an "analogous" color scheme by selecting one of the primary colors and using the two colors that are adjacent to it on the wheel. Another method is to choose any two colors that are opposite each other on the wheel to create a "complementary" color scheme. Complementary colors, when placed side by side, become more intense and exciting. The third basic method of combining colors is to use a "triad" of any three colors that are connected by the large triangles within the circle of the color wheel. Triads can include the three primary colors, the three secondary colors, or two sets of the three tertiary colors.

– THE SYMBOLIC USE OF COLOR –

In addition to the many ways we respond to color in nature, we also respond to the symbolic use of color. Different colors symbolize diverse ideas in different cultures. The Christian Church assigns colors to each season of the liturgical year. The color for Advent is a dark blue-purple, Lent is a clear hue of purple, white is for Christmas and Easter, red is for Pentecost, and green is for Trinity and Epiphany. The Native American also used color to symbolize his mystical nature, with red being the color for the sun god, black the color for the underworld god, and multicolor for the fire god. To the Chinese, colors represent the five elements—yellow for earth, black for water, red for fire, green for wood, and white for metal.

The meanings attributed to color can change not only from culture to culture, but also from one generation to another. Today, colors have a wide range of meanings that convey a variety of messages. White represents purity, as in "as pure as the driven snow." Yellow can symbolize cowardice, as in the expression "yellow-bellied," or it can be symbolized in a positive way as well. Examples can be found in two songs, "Tie a Yellow Ribbon 'Round the Old Oak Tree" and "The Yellow Rose of Texas." Red can be either joyful or angry, and a red rose symbolizes true love. Blue and green are peaceful colors, with blue as a symbol for heaven and green as a symbol for earth. Blue can also symbolize a sad or gloomy mood, as in "having the blues." Green can mean that one is inexperienced at certain tasks.

When we take all of the aspects of color into consideration, it is no wonder that choosing colors for a quilt is difficult. Using all of the methods of working with color in one quilt would create a haphazard, discordant mass of color that could detract from the other, unified elements.

Effective and unusual combinations can be found in many places, particularly if one considers the symbolic nature of color as well as the symbolic use of form. A trip to an art gallery to study color combinations in paintings or watercolors, both new and old, is a good resource for the contemporary quiltmaker. A relaxing afternoon spent listening to music can conjure up a vast array of color harmonies. Perhaps the best source of combining effective and unusual color combinations, however, is our own imaginations as we become more aware of the wealth of color in our natural surroundings.

Fig. 1 Grandmother's Mosaic, *mandala wall quilt, by*
Mary Ann Johnson, Boulder, Colorado.
Photo by the artist

Fig. 2 Dancing Tulips, *stained-glass appliqué quilt,*
by the author. Pattern in Chapter 12.
Photo by Alysoun Powell

Fig. 4 Circle of Friends, *by Julie Goodman, Fayetteville, Arkansas. Photo by Alysoun Powell*

Fig. 3 Bravissimo, *medallion quilt with a musical theme, by Deanna Powell, Melbourne, Florida. Photo by Bill Powell*

Fig. 5 Black, *a cruciform mandala in a striking setting, by Julie Goodman, Fayetteville, Arkansas. Photo by Alysoun Powell*

Fig. 6 English Garden, *medallion quilt in a simple square-on-square setting, by the author.*

Fig. 8 Star Paisley, *wall hanging based on a nine-patch quilt block, by the author. Pattern in Chapter 12.*

Fig. 7 Arbor Vitae, *a "Tree of Life" quilt, by the author. Pattern in Chapter 12. Collection of Patty and Charlie Ring, Palm Beach Gardens, Florida.*

Fig. 9 Counterpoint in Burgundy, *a large medallion quilt,*
by Marjorie Payne, Winter Haven, Florida.

Fig. 10 Sky Rocket Variation, *wall hanging*
based on a traditional pattern,
by Jennifer Collins, Tequesta, Florida.

Fig. 11 Aloha Angelica, *Hawaiian quilt, by Deanna Powell,*
Melbourne, Florida. Photo by Bill Powell

AT RIGHT:
Fig. 14 Cameo Rose, *making use of a natural mandala form,*
by Judy Simmons, Coral Springs, Florida.

Fig. 12 Priori, *a wall quilt with the Biblical account of Creation as a theme, by the author.*

Fig. 13 Mariner's Delight, *with shells used for quilting motifs. Made by the author as a wedding gift for Katherine Ward. Photo by Alysoun Powell*

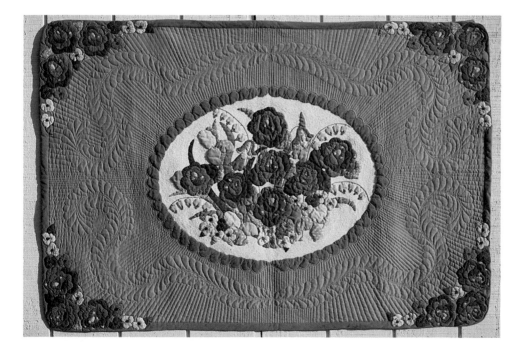

Fig. 15 Iris, *a small mandala wall quilt, by the author. Pattern in Chapter 12. Photo by Alysoun Powell*

Fig. 16 Dervish Star Medallion, *integrating the mandala design in both pattern and quilting motif, by Pat Reid, Merritt Island, Florida.*

Fig. 17 Mexican Star, *wall quilt of nine traditional blocks, by Kaye Connell, Jupiter, Florida.*

Fig. 18 Cockscombs and Currants, *a traditional appliqué pattern in a mandala design. Pattern in Chapter 12. Collection of Patti Irwin, Lake Park, Florida.*

Fig. 19 Evening Star, *a traditional star pattern in a mandala format. Pattern in Chapter 12. Collection of Katherine Ward, Palm Beach Isles, Florida. Photo by Alysoun Powell*

Fig. 20 Navajo Princess, *a contemporary setting for the traditional "Princess Feather" quilt block, by the author. Pattern in Chapter 12. Collection of Bill and Sally Gervin, Lake Park, Florida. Photo by Alysoun Powell*

Fig. 21 Sunrise, *a symbolic quilt made by a Sioux Indian woman in 1925. Collection of Charlene Robbin, Miami.*

Fig. 22 On the Wings of Morning, *a quilt design inspired by a theme from the Psalms, by the author.*

THE MANDALA
TRADITION

The craft of quilting originated in the Far East and was introduced in Northern Europe with the return of the Crusaders in the twelfth century. The Crusaders also brought with them many examples of Eastern art, some of which were based on mandala designs. From the beginning of time, artists have used symbols such as the mandala to express their response to their environment and to reveal their spiritual development. Even colonial women used the mandala design format as the central motif in medallion quilts, and contemporary quiltmakers today are carrying on the tradition.

In its most elemental form, the mandala is a simple circle. The circle can be divided into sections by placing the center design on a square within a square (Figure 4–1). Some mandalas have no circle at all, but use one or both of two other simple geometric

Fig. 4–1 The basic shapes of a mandala—the circle, square, and cross.

Fig. 4–2 Two examples of a cruciform mandala. LEFT, Maltese cross; RIGHT, Jerusalem cross.

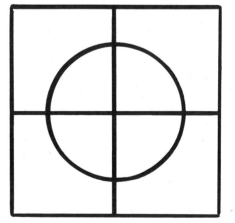

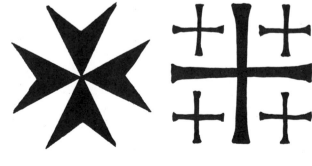

shapes—the square and the cross. These two shapes can be incorporated into an endless variety of designs to make mandala quilts. Many stitching techniques, such as piecing, appliqué, embroidery, stenciling, and trapunto, can be used in making medallion quilts, and of course you can make the mandala design as simple or as complex as you wish.

The mandala design is found throughout history in all civilizations. Most of the available information describes mandalas in the context of sacred images, although they are not exclusively used in this manner. In India and the Far East, the four- or eight-rayed circle is a common pattern found in religious articles used for meditation. Here the mandala usually represents the relationship of the universe to a spiritual power.

The mandala design is found in the mosaic floor designs of centuries-old Jewish temples in Israel. Stonehenge in England and many other neolithic standing stones in Great Britain are laid out in a mandala format. The mandala is found in abstract circular designs on the walls of early Christian churches in Rome. The mandala is used extensively in the Christian tradition in the form of a cross or cruciform, a primary symbol of faith. The equilateral Jerusalem and Maltese crosses are ancient symbols of the church. The Latin cross with the horizontal bar raised upward was introduced at a much later date.

Medieval medallions often show Christ in the center of an eight-rayed circle. The mandala design can also be found in paintings with Christ in the center, surrounded by the four evangelists. Stained-glass artists frequently use the mandala format in their designs. The mandala can be found in magnificent form in the famous rose windows of Europe's churches and cathedrals.

Mandalas can also symbolize a relationship between mankind and nature or between mankind and God. To many civilizations, the circle contains mystical powers, so it is sometimes referred to as a magic circle.

The mandala design was being used in America long before the first Europeans traveled to this continent. Native Americans have a longstanding tradition of using the mandala design in creating their spiritual images. In its most well-known form, it is the design used in creating the Navajo sand paintings of the Southwest. These sand paintings are a series of sacred images used to bring a person who is ill back into harmony with nature. The Indian believes that a lack of centeredness is the cause of illness. A sand painting is created specifically for the sick person, using symbols that

Fig. 4–3 Embroidered quilt in a mandala design. Collection of Diane Harris, Miami.

Fig. 4–4 Shadowbox Mandala, *a square-on-square mandala, by Lois Collins, Miami.*

have meaning in that person's life. The Navajos believe that the sand painting is filled with mystic power and therefore cannot be preserved. After it has served its purpose, it must be returned to the earth.

The circle also symbolizes a search for a purposeful, centered life. Quakers practice a form of meditation called *centering down,* which brings inner peace to those who master it. In meditation, a mandala represents the wholeness of life and the relationship of the universe to a spiritual power.

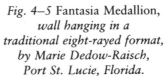

Fig. 4–5 Fantasia Medallion,
wall hanging in a
traditional eight-rayed format,
by Marie Dedow-Raisch,
Port St. Lucie, Florida.

Fig. 4–6 Mandala design based
on a traditional
"Little Giant" quilt block.

Fig. 4–7 Millrine Cross, *a contemporary quilt design based on a cruciform mandala, by Heidi Eitel.*

The geometric shapes that radiate from the center of a mandala can be figurative or abstract. In quilting, the mandala is represented abstractly in many of the traditional geometric, pieced block patterns, and figuratively through the wonderful old appliqué patterns, particularly floral designs.

The circle, the square, and the cross are the three most common geometric forms used in creating a mandala design, and a mandala often contains all three of these forms. Usually, emphasis is placed on the circle, which is then divided into four major sections. A quilt can be further divided into eight or sixteen sections. The four major sections usually represent the four cardinal points of the compass. They can also represent the cycles of life and death, the natural environment, or the sun, moon, stars, and heavenly bodies found in swirling galaxies that stretch through the vast reaches of space. Finally, the circle is placed within a square, which represents Earth, our own island home.

The quilt entitled *English Garden* (see color section, Figure 6) is made entirely in the square-within-a-square format. This format is repeated in the outer borders of the quilt, as well as in the center. Most medallion quilts include a series of stitched or printed borders that act as a frame for the finished piece. In *English Garden*, several of these borders have been pieced together to create a simple but effective pattern.

DESIGNING
MANDALA QUILTS

–CHOOSING A THEME–

Many themes can be expressed in a mandala design. The magic circle you design can symbolize the cycle of life and death, as in the popular "Tree of Life" pattern in antique quilts. The tree as a symbol for life originates in the second chapter of Genesis. Even a young child can picture a tree of life that emerges from the earth with branches reaching toward the heavens, while the roots that give it life and strength reach deep into the ground. The line of the horizon stretches both to the right and left to complete the mandala. The center of the mandala in the "Tree of Life" design is the point where the tree emerges from the earth. The "Tree of Life" is a good example of an asymetrical mandala form found in nature. *Arbor Vitae* (see color section, Figure 7), a "Tree of Life" quilt designed and made for Patty and Charlie Ring of Palm Beach Gardens, Florida, symbolizes the renewal of life.

STAR PATTERNS -- Another theme for a mandala quilt is the order of the universe, which can be interpreted as a mandala in a variety of forms. The most popular is expressed in star patterns. The quilted wall hanging *Star Paisley* (see color section, Figure 8) contains an intricate star that gives emphasis to the larger star in the center and is highlighted by smaller stars. It symbolizes the fullness of the heavens and all the stars that can be seen on a clear night. A quilt that has a similar pattern is *Counterpoint in Burgundy* (see color section, Figure 9), made by Marjorie Payne of Winter Park, Florida. Marjorie designed the center star and included some Chinese fabric, which gives the quilt an Oriental Flair.

Any book of quilt patterns will be filled with a large variety of stars, from just a simple star layout to extremely complex, multipieced blocks. Even a simple design can be effective. If you choose a star pattern for a quilt, you can build a design in a medallion around it. Jennifer Collins of Tequesta, Florida, used this approach when she designed her wall hanging, *Sky Rocket Variation* (see color section, Figure 10). She expanded the block and used a variety of unusual prints with one solid fabric for the finished piece.

SPIRITUAL THEMES -- The spiritual nature of the human experience can easily be depicted in a mandala format. A wonderful example on this Theme, *Aloha Angelica* (see color section, Figure 11), was made by Deanna Powel, an outstanding contemporary quilt artist. The blue she chose for the background is a perfect color to represent

Fig. 5–1 Blazing Star *block, pieced by Annette Stubbs, North Palm Beach.*

Fig. 5–2 Tora's Star, *quilt by*
Tora Sterregaard, Phoenix, Arizona.

the heavens. The four large angels in the center are bordered by a host of angels holding hands around the outside edges of the quilt.

Many antique quilts were designed around the four seasons or the four primal elements—earth, water, air, and fire—as in *Priori* (see color section, Figure 12). The "Storm at Sea" block in the center symbolizes the water that covered the earth prior to Creation, as described in Genesis I. The beige areas surrounding the center symbolize the arid desert described in the Creation story of Genesis II. The stars in the border are a traditional block called "World Without End." They are joined together to show the vastness of the heavens surrounding the earth. The red borders are symbolic of fire. The black border print that divides the beige areas represents the wailing wall in Jerusalem.

"MARINER'S COMPASS" -- Perhaps the most popular mandala design in quilts is the "MARINER'S COMPASS" pattern, which depicts the four cardinal points of the compass—North, East, South, and West. *Mariner's Delight* (see color section, Figure 13) is a variation on this pattern.

Some quiltmakers working in this design further divide the compass into as few as eight or as many as sixty-four sections. Many compass patterns are availabe for the quiltmaker to select from.

Stars are frequently used to fill in the surrounding areas of "Mariner's Compass" quilts. The "Mariner's Compass" quilt pattern "*Syzygy*" (see Figure 5–3) is perfectly balanced in design with the ocean waves at the bottom and the blowing winds at the top. A trip to the West Coast during a particularly stormy winter provided the inspiration for this pattern.

For other themes for a mandala quilt, look to nature and, more specifically, to your garden. Imagine either a full bouquet of flowers or a single blossom unfolding in a spiral pattern.

The rose is considered to be the perfection of the magic circle in nature. Judy Simmons used many roses in her quilt *Cameo Rose* (see color section, Figure 14), each one forming a perfect mandala. *Iris* (see color section, Figure 15), a small quilted wall hanging, displays a simple mandala format. Chapter 12, "Patterns and Projects," includes a number of patterns based on flower themes. Hawaiian quilt patterns, such

Fig. 5—3 Syzygy, *a pattern for a small wall hanging, illustrates different quilting motifs.*
(Pattern in Chapter 12.)

as that shown in Figure 5–4, are also excellent examples of nature represented through a mandala design. Microscopic images of snowflakes or sea creatures, such as the nautilus shell (Figure 5–5) are other mandala designs found in nature.

– DESIGNING A MAGIC CIRCLE –

When you have selected a theme that you think will best show your quiltmaking talents, establish a center point for your magic circle. Remember that each mandala must contain a clearly visible center as the focal point of the completed design, as in Figure 5–8. This is true whether you plan to draft a perfectly balanced pattern or a less formal, asymmetrical design. The circle should be divided into equal parts radiating outward from the center point. A four- or eight-section division is the easiest to work with. Fold the paper pattern into the number of sections you have chosen and develop your design in one of the sections. It will then be easy to trace the design in the remaining sections of the circle.

After completing the center section, you can place the circle within a square to symbolize the four corners of the Earth. You could then add interest to your design by placing the square "on point" inside an even larger square to make a diamond (Figure 5–8). If you place the square on point, attach four large triangles to each side.

Fig. 5–5 The nautilus shell, a spiral mandala found in nature.

Fig. 5–6 A spiral mandala
design suitable for
an appliquéd quilt.

Fig. 5–7 A magic-circle
design with a clearly
established center point.

Fig. 5–8 Placing the mandala
in the center of a quilt,
with the square "on point,"
bordered with a frame.

These triangles can be pieced, appliquéd, or simply quilted with an interesting motif that would further enhance the central design. Borders of printed fabric and additional rows of piecing or appliqué will add further interest and frame your design.

– ELEMENTS OF DESIGN –

As you develop the design for your quilt, consider all the elements of design—color, line, form, balance, symmetry, repetition, and texture. In addition to these elements, a good design must convey a certain feeling of tension or energy. It should lead the

Fig. 5–9 "Geometric Star Mandala" incorporating a traditional pieced star pattern. Design by Heidi Eitel.

eye from one area of the quilt to another and impart a feeling of excitement to the viewer. *Dervish Star Medallion* (see color section, Figure 16), by Pat Reid of Merritt Island, Florida, was drafted in a workshop taught by Deanna Powell. Pat took a traditional pattern for the basis of her design and elongated it into a rectangular shape. She also carries out the mandala concept in the quilting, which radiates from the center in dramatic lines to the outer edges.

Fig. 5–10 "Dresden Star Mandala" using two traditional patterns to produce a unified design quilt.

As you design your magic circle, expect it almost to take on a life of its own. The elements of your design should create a sense of harmony that extends throughout the quilt. The patterns of color and form should flow gracefully from the center, moving the eye first in one direction and then in another. Be careful that your center section doesn't become a "bull's eye" that will detract from the whole quilt. The final borders should be as integral to your overall design as the more important center section.

A well-designed magic-circle quilt should engage the imagination of both the maker and the viewer. A mandala should take us on a spiritual journey that encourages us to look both beyond and into ourselves to discover an element of mystery in our being. Ultimately, creating a mandala quilt, with its emphasis on the center with all other forms flowing out from it, should evoke a feeling of inner peace.

CREATIVE
QUILTMAKING

Today's quiltmakers are extending the traditions of the past and discovering that there is more to their craft than a temporary solution to the rainy-day blues. A great deal of craft work in the past seems to have been done for recreation, but now the "busy hands" attitude so often attributed to quilters is being replaced by a more serious approach to quilting as a folk art. For this reason, a new emphasis is being placed on the quality of work by contemporary quilt artists. Dedicated quilters with a desire to express what is important to them are taking a more thoughtful approach to each new fabric creation as they cut and stitch from their fabric palettes.

The question of whether quiltmaking is an art or a craft is frequently debated by today's quiltmakers. This question can be answered only by each quiltmaker as she pursues a standard of excellence in her own work. If a quiltmaker approaches her work with an interest in repeating the patterns of the past, then she may consider herself to be more of a craftswoman than an artist. However, the quiltmaker who is actively involved in discovering new skills and designing new quilt patterns should be recognized as both a craftswoman and an artist. All quiltmakers who are dedicated to preserving the folk art and craft of quiltmaking, whatever their individual approach may be, are making valuable contributions for new generations of quilters.

Regardless of whether you consider quiltmaking an art or a craft, it should be more than just a project to fill spare time. Instead, it should become an exciting creative process of discovering the many ways fabrics and patterns can be combined to make utilitarian bed coverings, decorative wall hangings, or masterpiece quilts. As today's quiltmakers piece together scraps of fabric with ever-improving design and stitching techniques, they are engaged in a centuries-old creative process.

It is clear that our ancestors stitched quilts out of necessity. Women in colonial America perfected this native folk art more than three centuries ago. The severe winter

Fig. 6–1 Carolina, *quilt by author in a "Sunburst" block,
a traditional magic-circle design.*

cold forced them to save every scrap of fabric and recycle the scraps into warm bed coverings. Nothing quite like the American quilt can be found in other countries or cultures. This unique folk art has now spread throughout the world, and quilt artists from many countries are coming to America to learn more about this craft.

The first quilts in America were pieced together as "crazy quilts" in order to use all available materials. As fabrics became easier to obtain, quilting became a way for

Fig. 6–2 Feathered Star, *by Annette Stubbs, North Palm Beach.*

women to express their individual creativity. As America grew, wealthier women could afford to purchase elaborately printed imported fabrics from India or the Far East. These fabrics were printed with birds, flowers, or figures, which often were cut out and appliquéd on a large piece of fabric in a technique called *broderie perse* and offered a more decorative approach to quilt design. Occasionally, the entire piece of patterned fabric would be quilted into whole-cloth, or counterpane, quilts (see Chapter 10). These printed fabrics were highly prized by quiltmakers in the eighteenth and nineteenth centuries. Women who could not afford to buy imported print fabrics were not discouraged by their lack of resources but, instead, were inspired by these richly patterned fabrics to create their own patterns with the technique of appliqué.

– APPLIQUÉ –

Appliqué involves cutting out free-form shapes from a piece of fabric and laying them on top of another piece of fabric with small, invisible hemming stitches. Many contemporary quiltmakers avoid appliqué because it may seem tedious. Like any other technique in stitching, however, appliqué becomes easier to execute with practice. Appliqué is an important technique in that it frees the quilt artist from the confinement of straight lines and simple geometric shapes and allows her to design from her imagination rather than from a pattern.

For centuries, women have devoted a considerable amount of time and energy to developing their needle skills, with the most accomplished stitchers being held in high esteem. These women have given contemporary quiltmakers a rich heritage of appliqué designs to draw from. A study of the techniques used as they worked to master their stitching reveals the legacy of excellence in workmanship, and one that is worthy of emulation and preservation.

Appliqué quilts designed in the medallion or mandala style enjoyed a surge of popularity in the late eighteenth and early nineteenth centuries, and today they are being re-created by contemporary quiltmakers. The patterns in Chapter 12 all use the magic-circle concept and can be used either as the center for a medallion quilt or as a group of mandala blocks in a more traditional design.

– TRADITIONAL QUILT BLOCKS –

Some well-known traditional quilt blocks that use the mandala as a design format are the "Feathered Star," "Mexican Cross," "Album Block," "Single Wedding Ring," "Mariner's Compass," "Princess Feather," "Coxcombs and Currants," "World Without End," and the "Carpenter's Wheel." If someone were to conduct a poll of quilters,

Fig. 6–3 "Feathered Star" quilt, late nineteenth century.

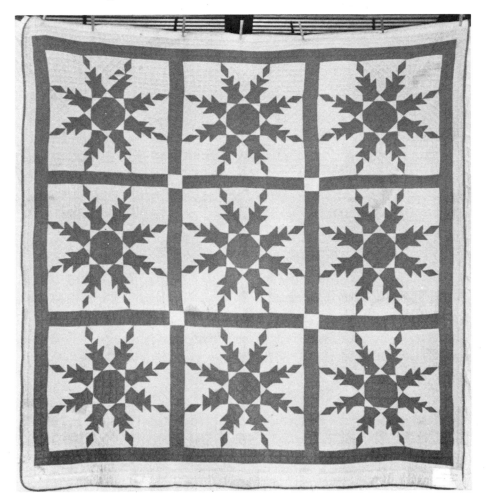

Fig. 6–4 *"Album Block" quilt in a cruciform mandala design.*

Fig. 6—5 "Single Wedding Ring" quilt in a square mandala shape.

asking them to name their favorite block, "Feathered Star" would be near the top of the list. It is one of many traditional blocks that have magic-circle beginnings. *Star of Roses* (see cover) is a small wall hanging made from this traditional pattern, but it is placed in an original setting and uses an unusual combination of fabrics to give it a distinct personality.

The "Mexican Cross" block is another excellent example of the mandala influence on traditional quilt blocks. Kaye Connell of Jupiter, Florida, made nine of these wonderful blocks, assembled them block to block, and surrounded them with a romantic chintz border print for her wall hanging entitled *Mexican Star* (see color section, Figure 17).

Antique quilts are wonderful sources when looking for magic-circle quilt designs. *Coxcombs and Currants* (see color section, Figure 18) is a handsome example owned by Patti Irwin of Lake Park, Florida, made by her grandmother in red and green. Our quilting ancestors were innovative in their use of the patterns that were available to them, and frequently they devised their own variations of traditional quilt blocks. Katherine Ward of Palm Beach Isles, Florida, has in her collection a scrap quilt entitled "Evening Star" that was made in the 1930s in Maine (see color section, Figure 19). It appears to be a combination of at least two old blocks, "Snowball" and "World Without End." This block may have been a pattern that was available during the 1930s, when quilting was enjoying a renaissance.

The craft of sewing scraps of plain or printed fabrics together by piecing geometric shapes, or the application of one piece of fabric on top of another to form new patterns, such as flowers, birds, or animals, has endured the test of time. It is during this process of creating a new piece of patterned fabric that quiltmakers move from making quilts as a simple craft and become quilt artists. Don't be discouraged if your first efforts in design seem to be primitive. Instead, look back once more to the antique quilts that inspire you and realize that you are in good company.

Practicing quiltmaking techniques and mastering the intricacies of appliqué is as enjoyable as it is rewarding. With each new project, try to experiment by selecting unusual fabrics and colors that will stretch your creativity. Participating in the quiltmaking tradition by making familiar patterns is an equally valuable learning exercise, but it should not keep you from exploring new possibilities. Studying the history of quiltmaking will lead to the wonderful discovery that our quiltmaking ancestors were not as devoted to preserving tradition as we might think. Indeed, they were quite

Fig. 6–6 Mandala combining a "Pieced Star" block and "Jack-in-the-Box" block.

*Fig. 6–7 A mandala quilt design based on
traditional quilt blocks, by Heidi Eitel.*

innovative in their approach to their quiltmaking tasks. If they had not been, we would not have a resource of more than 4,000 traditional quilt blocks to draw from.

–PLANNING THE DESIGN–

Many of today's quiltmakers are striving to continue the tradition of making masterpiece quilts. Developing a design for a masterpiece quilt requires a commitment of

Fig. 6–8 "Egyptian Star Blossom Mandala," combining the techniques of piecing, appliqué, and quilting.

time and energy. A good way to begin an original quilt design is to sketch a favorite traditional quilt block. Draft the block on a piece of graph paper and then stretch your imagination to see how you can make the shapes and forms grow. Expect to use several sheets of paper as you plan your quilt. Lightly shade in the shapes with a pencil, remembering that the use of light, medium, and dark values will enhance the overall impact of your design. You may want to experiment with various arrangements of values as you plan your work. When you finally settle on a design, you will experience a wonderful feeling of satisfaction for your efforts.

The next step is to draft the full-size pattern in order to prepare your templates.

Fig. 6–9 Calico Star Mandala, *combining two traditional quilt blocks, by Lois Collins, Miami.*

A word of warning: Don't be tempted to cut the entire quilt at one sitting. You will want to be free to make changes in your design as you make each new section. Begin with the center block, cut and stitch the pieces, and then study the results before going on to the next section. As you work, you will discover that the quilt will take on a unique personality of its own.

Refer to your plan, but do not feel bound to it. Be willing to alter the plan at any point along the way. Work the quilt out to the final borders in this manner. You cannnot be anxious about the investment of time that is necessary to make a quilt of this quality or you will begin to take shortcuts that will detract from your original purpose. Keep in mind that you are making a quilt that will be cherished by future generations.

Contemporary quiltmakers are discovering the joy in quiltmaking that comes from designing and making a quilt that is uniquely their own. Innovative quilt design can take you on an exciting artistic journey as the creative process unfolds. Think of using fabric, batting, and thread as a sculptor uses stone or a painter uses pigment. Ideas for putting fabric, color, and form together can be found in many sources. Look around you for ideas for incorporating color, shape, and movement in your design. You may want to tell a story about your dreams, your lifestyle, or your environment.

Literature provides a vast array of images that can be interpreted with fabric and thread. Select what appeals to you and create your own interpretation. Consider the mandala and the magic circle an exciting design format for your quilt, to convey messages to future generations of quilters through contemporary or traditional symbols.

Finally, choose a color or pattern that will give your quilt a unique personality. That unattractive fabric that is in the quilt-shop sale section may be just the piece to give your quilt individuality. Step out of manufactured fabric groupings and traditional small calico prints to make your own unique combinations of patterns and fabrics. Buy only good-quality fabric and batting. Cotton fabrics are the easiest to work with, but choose a blend if a particular color or print appeals to you.

Finish your quilt top with quilting designs that will enhance and complement your piecing or appliqué. Do not neglect this wonderful textural element. Exciting things can happen during the quilting process to give your work a special quality. Embellishments of embroidery, old lace or buttons, ribbons, and other trims can add a personal touch to a quilt project. Quilting provides creative opportunities that are limited only by the imagination of the individual quiltmaker.

FROM ORDINARY TO EXTRAORDINARY

Like most quilters, when I first became a quiltmaker, every quilt I saw was an exciting visual experience. But as I attended more and more quilt shows, my eye became increasingly discriminating, and many of the quilts seemed to become less and less exciting. My first reaction to this observation was that I must have seen all the "good" quilts in the first few shows I attended. Then I eventually realized that I had simply become a more educated and selective viewer.

As I became more discerning, I realized that some quilts have an impact. They draw you into them and make you curious about the design and technique employed by the quiltmaker. Another interesting discovery was that some of the quilts that possessed a lot of razzle-dazzle when I first saw them lost some of their appeal as I studied the quality of craftsmanship, both in construction and in the quilting. I found that many of the quilts that employed a sophisticated but subtle use of color and design held my attention and admiration the longest. They were the quilts I kept going back to see again and again, and it was exciting to find some new fabric, line, or technique each time I returned.

I finally started to study the qualities that made some quilts ordinary and others extraordinary. This more seasoned approach to looking at quilts led me to the conclusion that some quilts are simply poorly stitched or the materials poorly chosen. Some quilts are well constructed and made of good materials but lack of a certain quality of design that could enhance their overall appearance. Two areas in which otherwise well-made quilts seem to lack imagination are in the method used to set the blocks together and the surface design of the quilting motifs. I began to wonder why a quiltmaker who obviously spent hours of careful work in piecing blocks or stitching subtly curving appliqué did not follow through by devising creative settings or interesting quilting motifs.

*Fig. 7–1 "Mandala Maze," a contemporary mandala design
using traditional strip-piecing techniques, by Heidi Eitel.*

– STUDYING TECHNIQUES IN ANTIQUE QUILTS –

In looking for answers to this question, I studied old quilts that caught my attention and intrigued me enough to bring me back to look at them over and over again. I concluded that our quilting ancestors must not have felt as bound by rules for putting their quilts together as many contemporary quiltmakers seem to be. Their limited resources forced them to be more resourceful in their designs. Whatever the reason, quilters of yesteryear employed a variety of techniques for setting their blocks into quilts. They used pieced sashing, oversize chintz fabrics for lattice, and zigzag settings, or they alternated their pieced or appliqué blocks with solid or chintz fabric squares in diagonal settings. Sometimes they pieced their borders together in designs that not only complemented the finished quilt blocks but also gave an exciting secondary movement to the pieced or appliqué pattern.

Many of the old medallion quilts featured rows of stars in borders surrounding the center design or wide muslin borders that were used to display intricate quilting motifs. The makers of these antique quilts frequently used curved or appliqué pieces in the borders of geometrically pieced medallion quilts to give relief to the straight lines employed in the center portion of the quilt. "The Orange Peel," "Robbing Peter to Pay Paul," and swag-and-tassle appliqué borders were favorites.

Discovering all this has led me to pretend occasionally that the fabrics I have in my workroom are all that are available to me. I imagine that I am living in an isolated log cabin and can use only the supplies that I have on hand. Playing this little game forces me to work out new solutions for putting quilts together. It also forces me to be much more creative in my selection and use of color. This is because one of the rules of this game prohibits me from running down to the corner quilt store to match perfectly a favorite piece of calico.

After selecting a block pattern (my favorite block is the "Ohio Star"), I search through my fabrics for a workable color combination. I am stockpiling a collection of cotton fabrics in my closet just in case there is a fabric famine in the future. This imagined fear that I may someday be unable to get supplies has led me to purchase a working treadle sewing machine to use during tropical storms. (A dedicated quiltmaker should be prepared for all such emergencies!)

If you are a seasoned quiltmaker and keep stashes of fabric in your closet and under your bed, you probably will have no trouble finding fabric for the smaller squares and triangles of a pieced block or for the petals of appliqué flowers. However, I have discovered that my habit of purchasing two-yard cuts of fabrics that are especially appealing to me is often limiting when I begin to make a new quilt, since most quilts have lattices and outer borders that are usually longer than six feet. Few quilts are needed on beds in a tropical climate, so I usually make small quilts or wall hangings instead.

After the quilt top is complete, the next step is the quilting process itself. Too many contemporary quiltmakers view the quilting process as merely a means of holding the top, the batting, and the backing together when this should be the most exciting part of the entire project. The textural dimension that the quilting process adds to the quilt design is what excites the educated viewer the most. Stitching the quilt together a quarter of an inch inside each seam line using a natural colored thread is too ordinary a finish for a well-planned quilt. A study of old quilts will show that they were frequently quilted without any regard to seam lines. Instead, the quilting traveled in geometric or curved lines across the surface of the quilt, creating an appealing contrapuntal effect. It was common to use flowing lines on the surface of a geometric quilt and straight lines over appliqué designs.

If you intend to invest hours of time in making a quilt, then you should also plan to invest an equal amount of time in planning unique and unusual settings and quilting motifs. And if you are willing to piece together a series of blocks in intricate patterns, you should also be willing to piece together lattices to set the blocks. An outstanding appliqué design should be complemented by a well-planned appliqué border motif to frame the central area. In the same manner, if you have invested a substantial amount of time and effort in the planning and sewing of the quilt top, you should follow through with the same diligence for the quilting stitches. There is no rule that says you must not stitch across seam lines in a pieced quilt or over the top of an appliqué design if the stitching enhances the overall appearance of the quilt.

As you plan your next quilt, make the journey from the ordinary to the extraordinary. Use antique quilts that are unique in design and technique as your road maps. Then experiment until you are confident that you have selected the elements of design that will best interpret your ideas.

Fig. 7–2 The traditional "Bird's Nest" quilt block was the basis
for this contemporary mandala design by Heidi Eitel.

Today, since quiltmakers have so many wonderful fabrics, patterns, and quilting-motif templates to choose from, the number of design approaches you can take is almost limitless.

– EXPANDING YOUR ARTISTIC HORIZONS –

Successful quiltmakers are frequently told how lucky they are to have been born with all that wonderful talent. A quilter certainly has an edge if she possesses some inherent talent and a finely developed sense of color. However, we all have a certain amount of potential that enables us to make beautiful quilts if we are willing to work at developing the skills we already possess, and the eye can be trained to perceive design elements and learn the rules of color design.

A talented musician, actor, or dancer must study for years and practice diligently if he or she wants to achieve success and recognition. This same dedication and discipline must be followed by the quilt artist. One way to become a better quilt artist is to attend quilt workshops and seminars. You can learn the elements of design and how to use color effectively in a variety of classroom and workshop situations. If you are unable to attend a quilting retreat, investigate the curriculum offered in adult-education classes at local schools, colleges, or art galleries. Serious quiltmakers should look for classes that offer a general art education in addition to quiltmaking classes.

Always take the opportunity to explore new ideas and methods of working. Many of today's well-known quilt artists have some background in the fine arts. This background gives them an advantage, but it is one that everyone can obtain by taking classes in the visual arts. Taking a course in art history will familiarize the quiltmaker with the use of symbols and design in different cultures throughout history.

Workshops and seminars presented specifically for quiltmakers provide an opportunity for quilters at every level of accomplishment, from beginner to expert, to improve the quality of their work and learn exciting new techniques. They also provide an important opportunity for sharing ideas, getting inspiration for dozens of new quilts (most of which may never be made), and using rolls and rolls of color film. The only disadvantage of these seminars is that some quiltmakers return home only to imitate the work of the instructor, rather than put their new knowledge and techniques to work in their own way. It is easy to make a quilt or two in a style that has been presented in a workshop and then move to another seminar and repeat the process.

While quilt seminars and workshops are vital to quiltmakers who are anxious to learn new quilting techniques, each quiltmaker should try to develop an individual style for her own work. A two- or three-day workshop will not give you enough time, no matter how talented and inspiring the teacher is, to explore all the possibilities for using color, line, or design. These are skills that take months to develop and require the long-term guidance of a good instructor.

In addition to unraveling the mysteries of color, a class in basic design will teach the quiltmaker to reduce all forms, no matter how complex they may first appear to be, to the simplest of geometric forms. Here you will learn that the circle is one of the easiest geometric forms to use in the development of a well-balanced design. The magic circle can become an exciting possibility for myriad quilt designs.

Because so much time and money are involved in making a quilt, pursuing new skills and knowledge should be a top priority for all quiltmakers. Keep in mind how much time you have to devote to quiltmaking, and space classes to allow time for quilting as well as learning. Quilting should always be a joy and a challenge.

AN INDIVIDUAL
APPROACH TO
QUILTMAKING

Each quiltmaker who is dedicated to her craft has developed an individual approach over a period of time that is comfortable and productive for her. From time to time, I set aside my stitching for a few days to reflect on what I have produced in the past and where I might like to go in the future. Analyzing my own approach to the art of quiltmaking has become an integral part of my working style. The better I understand myself and what I am trying to interpret with my needle, thread, and fabric, the more satisfied I will be with the results of my efforts.

I see myself as a hopeless romantic with a well-developed mystical nature living in the age of science. The joy that comes from pulling threads from the past into a contemporary quilt with my needle is an immensely satisfying experience. I feel that I share a special kinship with all the women who have stitched before me. These women showed great creativity and ingenuity in developing techniques that we can all benefit from as we strive to take quiltmaking into new and uncharted areas. My hope is to add something to the craft of quiltmaking for future generations to enjoy and cherish. I would love to look down from heaven late in the next century to see my quilts being admired and studied by the quiltmakers of the future. I look not only to what is happening in quiltmaking today but also to the past as a way to expand my experiences in quilting.

When designing a quilt, I combine the techniques of piecing and appliqué because it gives me the most freedom in developing and interpreting my ideas. I try to draw from the past by beginning with a traditional block. Deanna Powell describes this method of designing as "going from traditional block to contemporary quilt." Using this approach, any traditional quilt block can be expanded and developed in a non-traditional setting that is limited only by the imagination of the individual quiltmaker.

One of my favorite methods of working is to appliqué a large center block and then surround it with an even larger pieced block, as in *Navajo Princess Quilt* (see color section, Figure 20). I drafted the princess feather design by combining ideas from several antique quilts that were especially appealing in both color and form. The original plan called for four large appliquéd feather motifs set together with a small pieced border in a traditional manner. After completing the appliqué of eight individual feathers into the circle, I abandoned the idea of stitching the additional three blocks. I set the block aside for several months while I pondered what to do with it. One day, while idly looking through a book of traditional quilt patterns, I was inspired by a Navajo block and decided to use it as a setting for the appliqué princess feather. I added a border to frame the design and give it a finished appearance. All the fabrics that I used in the center motif I also used in the pieced Navajo block and borders to give unity to the finished quilt.

I frequently become bogged down and set a quilt aside during the construction process. When this happens, I follow the rules of logic and work through the design problem. The first step is to define the problem. I begin by listing the things I like about the quilt and, more important, the things that are giving me the most difficulty. It is important to determine whether the problem is in fabric or color selection or in the construction or design. Next, I list all the possible solutions I can come up with from my experience. When this second list is complete, I enter the creative-thinking stage in the hope of finding a solution to the problem.

I keep paper and pencil on my bedside table to sketch any ideas that come to mind before I fall asleep so that I won't forget them while I do my morning housekeeping chores—although sometimes I am so excited about an idea that I go right to my sewing studio and neglect other duties. I compare my new ideas to the other solutions already on my list to test all the possibilities. Some of my best quilt designs evolved from this method. It also saves hours of frustration, stacks of paper, and yards of fabric that otherwise would have been wasted.

Perhaps my most important tool for creative problem solving is of my own making. The most significant thing I learned while majoring in art in college was the importance of keeping a sketchbook. We were required to make volumes of sketches each week, and our drawing pads were checked by our instructor. This instilled in me a habit of sketching any ideas that come to mind, whether or not I think they may be of use.

65

For a quilt sketchbook, keep a handy supply of graph paper and a pencil at all times or even a small pad of scored paper that fits into a purse. Jot down each idea as you see it, whether it is from a quilt show or from a mosaic design from a building entrance or floor. It is surprising how quickly these visual aids accumulate into a collection of possible solutions to future quilt-design problems. The sketch book will become a handy and invaluable reference.

Whenever you change the original plan of a quilt, you must have an ample supply of fabrics when you begin. Never cut the pieces for the entire quilt; cut only enough pieces to see if the fabrics will work together as planned. Sometimes fabrics that look good together on the bolt do not work well in a particular pieced or appliqué block. Once you have bought all the fabric for the quilt, you cannot make further changes. If the plan is not working, you may have to abandon the project altogether or put it aside until you find a solution to the problem. Working in this manner means that I often have several quilt projects in various stages of completion. Usually an upcoming quilt competition provides the necessary motivation to finish quilts on a regular basis.

When I make a mistake in a design, I usually fall back on my art school training and follow the old rule that says, "don't try to minimize a mistake in the hope that it won't show." This never works. The only creative solution to mistakes is to maximize them by adding something obvious. If you are working on a pieced quilt, add a touch of piecework that moves from the main area of the design to the outer borders. If you are appliquéing a quilt, you can always stitch a heart, a leaf, or a spray of flowers out into the border area for a finishing touch.

When I work out the assembly of individual patterns, I include a variety of construction techniques in each quilt. I find that using precision-cutting and machine-piecing techniques is the most efficient way to work. I often cut four layers of fabric at a time, using very sharp scissors or a rotary cutter. I save thread and cleanup time by feeding the pieces through the machine in sequence and clipping them apart when finished.

I use the sewing machine only for piecework because I prefer to have no machine stitching on the surface of the quilt. For this reason, I use hand appliqué and quilting techniques exclusively. Basting applique pieces is time-consuming, so I pin the pieces to the background fabric and turn the edges under with a needle as I stitch. The stitching should be invisible, so I frequently use one strand of embroidery floss for appliqué thread. It comes in a wide variety of colors and is fine enough to disappear into the seam line. Floss must be run over beeswax to strengthen it and prevent fraying. Curves and points are sculpted with the point of the needle just prior to stitching. For this method to be successful, you must carefully mark the pattern on the background fabric. This is easy to do with a homemade light table, which you can make by placing a lamp under a glass or clear plastic tabletop.

Each quiltmaker must develop a way of working that brings satisfaction and good results. Try new methods of working to see if they are right for you, and don't feel that you must work in a certain way because another quiltmaker has recommended it. The only right way to stitch is the way that works best for you.

QUILTING STITCHES: THE FINISHING TOUCH

"Is that all there is to it?" This is the comment most frequently heard in a beginning quilt class. There seems to be a mystique surrounding the quilting process that makes it appear to be more difficult than it really is. Quilting is quite simply a short running stitch that secures the quilt top, batting, and backing. The necessary equipment is also simple: All you need is a needle, some thread, a thimble, and patience.

Fig. 9–1 Basic quilting equipment.

– QUILTING MOTIFS –

Perhaps one aspect of quilting that does not seem to be simple is deciding what quilting motifs to use in different areas of each quilt. Quilting should be more that just the process of securing the three layers of fabric; it should also be an integral part of a total quilt design. The quilting stitches added to the surface of each quilt can give a quilt an added dimension and texture.

The imaginative use of line texture can create an exciting secondary element of design and movement on the surface of a completed quilt. The quilting stitches that are added to each quilt top can be an expression of each individual quilter's personality. They can tell whether or not a quilter enjoys the quilting process, and how much thought and importance she has given to the craft.

Considering how a quilt will be quilted is important to fabric selection, and the best time to think about this is during the planning stages of the project. The quilting motifs you choose also will have an effect on fabric selection, as well as on the size of sashings and borders and the selection and placement of settings for the pieced or appliqué block. Early planning of the quilting motifs is particularly important in medallion or magic-circle quilts because these quilts often contain large areas specifically intended for hand-quilting.

Unfortunately, the selection of quilting motifs that will provide an interesting counterpoint to the design of the quilt top is frequently ignored or added only as an afterthought in many contemporary quilts. Certainly the patchwork or appliqué must be carefully executed in each quilt, with great care being given to the selection of color, fabric, and pattern.

Your quilting stitches can easily be lost if they are done over a print fabric. For this reason, you may want to use solid fabrics for the quilting motifs. It is equally important during the design process to consider exactly how you will quilt the top. The introduction of polyester and bonded cotton batting has freed today's quiltmaker from the necessity of quilting closely to prevent wadding. However this does not mean that the quilting stitches should be taken lightly. It is very important to quilt evenly throughout the entire quilt top. The quilt should be consistent in the use of light, medium, or heavy quilting on all areas of the quilt top. Don't quilt heavily in the center section and then neglect surrounding areas or borders; it is amazing how many beautiful quilts are worked with care throughout, then neglected in the borders. A careful quilter will give the same loving attention to detail all the way out to the edges of the quilt top.

The next time you attend a quilt show, pay careful attention to the manner in which each quilt is quilted. One of the things you will notice is that on antique quilts it was customary to add curved quilting lines to geometric designs and straight lines to the curved patterns of appliquéd quilts. Elaborate quilting patterns were used to enhance the borders and sashings of even the most ordinary quilts. It is obvious that our quilting ancestors enjoyed the quilting process as a means of displaying their stitching skills.

– S T I P P L E Q U I L T I N G –

Another technique used by our quilting ancestors was *stipple quilting* (Figure 9–2). The work *stipple* has been borrowed from painters and describes the technique that artists use to make close, small, quick brushstrokes on the surface of a canvas. The term retains the same meaning when applied to the quilting process. Stippling is a

Fig. 9–2 An example of random stipple quilting.

method of stitching that involves making rows and rows of small, close, and sometimes random stitching. The stitches are usually about $\frac{1}{16}$ to $\frac{1}{8}$ inch apart, and they are used to fill in areas behind the principal quilting motifs. This flattens out the background fabric and "raises up" the quilt design that the stitcher wants to emphasize. If you are not comfortable enough in your quilting to make random stitches, even rows of cross-hatch stitching behind the curving lines of a larger quilting motif will provide the same effect (Figure 9–3).

When I first began quilting, I was more interested in selecting and putting together all the wonderful print fabrics I found than I was in quilting the finished quilt top. I saw quilting only as a necessary chore to finish a quilt project, and I actually dreaded stitching my first quilt. I soon discovered that quilting is an immensely satisfying experience. Now I can sit and quilt for hours each day, enjoying the soothing feel of the fabric and the peaceful rocking motion of the needle as it glides in and out of the layers of fabric.

I now enjoy quilting so much that I plan specific areas in each quilt for individually designed quilting motifs. I often take these motifs from a distinctive print fabric that begs to be used as a quilting motif as well as part of a pieced or appliqué block. I also use many commercial quilt templates. If I need a rose or feather motif, I trace parts of these templates onto the surface of the fabric, manipulating them to fit the areas that need to be quilted. It is important to have the quilting motifs relate in some way to the design of the quilt. The best way to learn how to select quilting motifs that will add an exciting textural element to a quilt design is through practice.

Each quilt can teach the stitcher something new about the quilting process and the selection of quilting designs for the next quilt project. By the time most quiltmakers have one quilt ready to be quilted, they have another in the planning stages. Make mental notes as you quilt about the things you are doing that work and, equally important, the things that don't work. Being a good quilter and quilt designer is not a talent you are born with, but rather a skill that you develop as you work on each new quilt.

– STITCHING ACROSS SEAM LINES –

It is surprising how many contemporary quilters assume there is a rule in quilting that says: *Never quilt across a seam line*. Actually, just the opposite is true if you base your

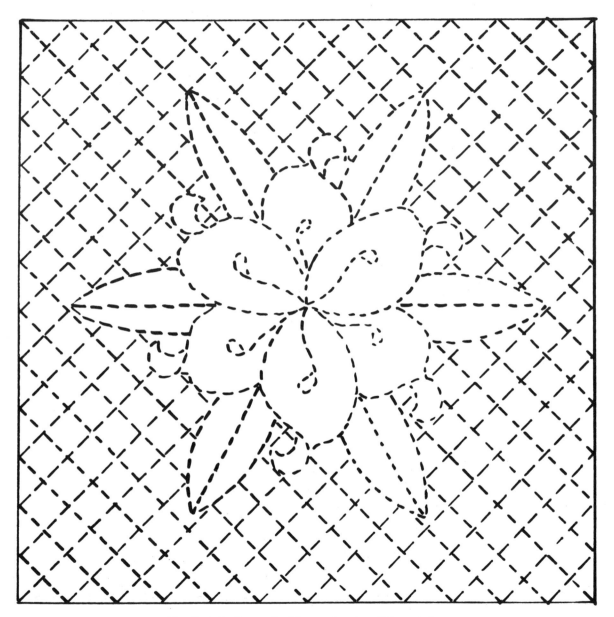

Fig. 9–3 Quilt motif with crosshatch quilting stitches.

quilting decisions on antique quilts. They were quilted evenly throughout the entire quilt top with little or no regard to seam lines. Quilting rigidly ¼ inch inside each seam line emphasizes the seams by creating little ridges along the line and little puckers where seams intersect. These ridges are more noticeable because of the extra fabric in the seam allowance that is pressed to one side, as is customary in quilting. Stitching across seam lines helps to keep the lines flat, especially where seams meet, and it gives the illusion that the quilt was made from a whole piece of cloth. This look is particularly desired when a quilt is set together with alternating squares of background fabric rather than sashing.

– NEEDLES AND THREAD –

When you have finally settled on the motifs you want to use, whether you have drawn them yourself or used commercial templates, you are ready to quilt. Perhaps some of the mystique of quilting is in the language that quilters use. They don't call their needles *needles*. They call them *betweens*. Betweens are shorter than ordinary sewing needles. Novice quiltmakers look at them and wonder how they ever go through all those layers of fabric and lining. Just remember that small needles make small stitches. Betweens come in several sizes; beginners usually start with size 9. Experienced quilters use size 10 or 12.

Since quilts are made to be used, quiltmakers usually select a stronger thread than ordinary sewing thread for the quilting. If you are making a decorative wall hanging, you may choose to use colored embroidery floss to add interest to your design. Quilting thread comes in a limited range of colors, but you should experiment with them. You may want to run your quilting thread or embroidery floss through beeswax to prevent twisting and knotting while you stitch.

– THIMBLES –

Thimbles are a must. If you have never sewn with the aid of a thimble, it will seem awkward at first. Be patient while you are learning to use it. The thimble is usually placed on the middle finger of your sewing hand. You will not be able to push the needle through all those layers of fabric and batting without a thimble. If you try, you will soon have a painful hole in your finger. Once you have mastered the use of a thimble, you will never again sew without one. I was forced into using a thimble over twenty years ago by an elderly aunt who taught me fine French hand sewing. She would not let me sew without one. I can remember sitting there in silent anger and frustration as I struggled to adapt to it. Now I cannot pick up a needle and thread unless I also have my thimble at hand.

– PREPARING TO QUILT –

To prepare your finished quilt top for the quilting process, begin by marking the quilting lines or quilt motifs on the quilt top. A variety of full-size motifs for blocks and borders are included in Chapter 11. They can be easily traced to your fabric by taping both fabric and drawing together and then placing them on a window or by using a home-made light table.

The next step is to baste together the quilt top, batting, and backing. This must be done so that the layers will not shift, fold, or pucker as you quilt. Lay the backing fabric with the wrong side facing up on the floor or large table. Smooth out all the wrinkles and tape the corners securely with masking tape. Place the batting on top of the backing fabric and again smooth out all wrinkles and lumps. The batting and backing should be a little larger (usually about two inches on each side) than the finished quilt top. Next, add the quilt top, carefully smoothing out all wrinkles one more time. When smoothing wrinkles, always start in the center and work out to the edges.

Begin basting with a long needle and baste with large stitches from the center out to the edges of the quilt. Make both a cross and a "X" (Figure 9–4). Baste also in both horizontal and vertical rows approximately six inches apart to secure the quilt layers. This is time-consuming and may seem like a waste of time, since all of the basting will be removed after the quilting is done. However, sloppy or inadequate basting will allow the layers to shift, and this will cause puckers in the finished quilt.

When you finish the basting, you can begin quilting. You will need to put your quilt in a large floor frame or use a large round or oval embroidery hoop to keep your

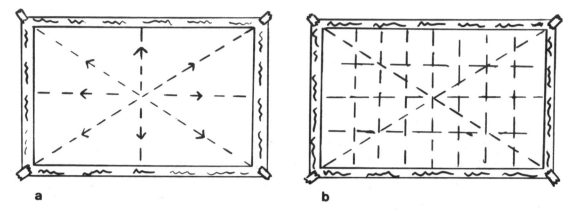

Fig. 9–4 Assembling the quilt. (a) STEP 1: Basting the quilt top, batting, and backing together. (b) STEP 2: Completing the basting with rows of horizontal and vertical stitches.

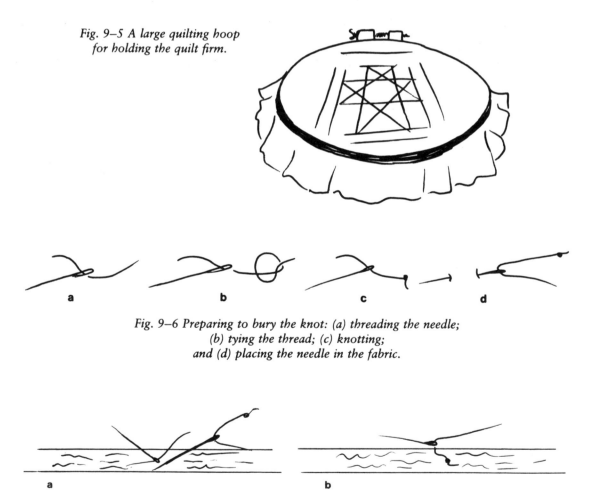

Fig. 9–5 A large quilting hoop for holding the quilt firm.

Fig. 9–6 Preparing to bury the knot: (a) threading the needle; (b) tying the thread; (c) knotting; and (d) placing the needle in the fabric.

Fig. 9–7 To bury the knot in the batting, and hold thread firmly in place: (a) slide and scoop the needle, then (b) tug and pop the knot to begin and end.

Fig. 9–8 The correct way to hold the needle when quilting.

work smooth and wrinkle-free while you stitch. Begin in the center of the quilt and work out to the edges. Don't worry about the size of your finished quilt and how long it will take to finish the stitching. Instead, strive to finish one "hoopful" of quilting each day. You will be surprised to see how quickly the stitching goes.

To begin quilting, cut a length of thread from 12 to 15 inches long and thread the needle. Tie a small knot in one end of the thread (Figure 9–6). The knot should be buried between the layers of batting and backing so that it won't show on the front or the back of the quilt. Slide your needle through the fabric and scoop up a little of the batting, and pull the needle up at the point where you plan to begin stitching (Figure 9–7A). Give the thread a firm tug to "pop" the knot through the top layer and into the batting (Figure 9–7B). Stitch along the marked lines with short running stitches that go through all the layers of fabric and batting. Position your thumb in front of the needle to guide the length of the stitch. Take several stitches at a time on your needle. It is more important that your stitches be even rather than small when you begin.

As you practice, you will gradually begin to make smaller stitches with little effort. Finish each length of thread by tying a small knot in the end of the thread near the fabric surface. Pop the knot one more time and bury it in the batting before snipping the tail off with scissors.

COUNTERPANE QUILTING DESIGNS

Counterpane quilting is an elegant form of quilting that is usually done with white thread on white fabric. Counterpane quilts are commonly referred to as whole-cloth quilts because they are made from one large piece of fabric. The motifs usually begin in the center and extend to the edges. There is no piecing or appliqué involved. Many antique counterpane quilts, often made of a fabric called linsey-woolsey and in colors such as red and blue, are elegant works of art that can challenge and inspire contemporary quiltmakers who are willing to take the time to study them carefully.

Quilters from the past gave their best efforts to counterpane quilting, and many of these quilts are elegant works of art. The first quilted counterpane designs were stitched in simple, straight lines in either diamonds or squares. Eventually, the motifs became more elaborate and included curved lines and swirls. Many of the patterns that became popular can be traced to specific geographical areas, where they were used for elaborate bed furnishings and clothing.

As quilting techniques were refined, other decorative effects were employed. *Stuffed work* is a technique used to enhance counterpane quilts, where elaborate quilting designs are stuffed with cotton wadding worked between the layers of the quilt. A flower, leaf, or feather could take on an almost sculptural effect when padded in this manner. A great deal of patience is required to part the woven threads of the backing fabric with a needle and then carefully push the wadding into the motif.

Trapunto is another technique for creating a raised or sculpted effect. This is done by threading a large needle with thick yarn and pushing the yarn between the layers from the back of the quilt. The needle and yarn are then forced to travel along the length of a quilted channel.

Quilting designs from colonial days are still in demand, and they offer an interesting contrast to contemporary geometric quilts. Feathers, flowers, birds, shells, fruit, and swirling geometric shapes all graced the quilts of our ancestors. Designs were available in the form of patterns that were stamped on paper or punched out in tin stencils. Many quilters, however, created their designs with rulers, teacups, or other household items. Today's quilters are fortunate to have a wealth of inexpensive, lightweight, and durable plastic templates to choose from for marking their finished quilt tops.

The success of the design of most contemporary quilts depends mostly on the fabric, color, and pattern selected by the individual quiltmaker. But the quilting process and the selection of quilting motifs or patterns can give the quilt an important added dimension—texture. Carefully planned quilting stitches executed in a fascinating counterpoint design of line and tension can set up an exciting secondary movement throughout the quilt and subtly enhance the overall design.

Perhaps we respond to the surface stitching on quilts because it appeals to a basic sensory response that all humans share—the sense of touch. No doubt all of us were wrapped in a quilt, either handmade or manufactured, then rocked and cuddled during our infancy. Perhaps this is where our emotional need to touch quilts began. My two daughters have handmade quilts that were stitched and given to them by their paternal grandmother before their births. They were both carried home from the hospital in their quilts, and the same quilts went to college with them.

Touch is important to a small child as a way of providing information to help develop coordination between the hand and the eye. Touch sensations give information to the brain that the eye alone cannot give. As a small child, I can remember slipping under a pink and white "Irish Chain" quilt that was one of a pair that my grandmother made for my mother. It is the only link I have with my grandmother, for she died before I was born. All I know of her is how comforting it was each night to be under the quilt she made. I picked at the yarn ties that held it together as I drifted off to sleep. It provided a "touch" between my grandmother and me that would not have been possible otherwise.

The sense of touch plays an important role in our physical and emotional lives. Quilting provides an exciting response to this basic human need. Sewing involves many specific touch sensations. During the hand-quilting process, we rely upon the sense of touch as we piece our fabrics or as we guide our needles up, down, and through the layers of fabric and batting.

The quilting motifs on the following pages, all full-size, have been developed to supplement the vast amount of traditional designs available to the quiltmaker. With the magic circle as a base, each one begins in the center with a basic concept and expands to the outer edges in a flow of circles, curves, and points. They can be stitched as individual samplers with a narrow-print border or used in larger quilts on alternating solid-color fabric blocks.

Many of the motifs are complemented by coordinating borders and small block designs. Some of the patterns are presented as block designs only. You can copy them easily on tracing paper and use them in any number of quilt layout designs. I look forward to seeing them stitched in quilts as I attend quilt shows in the future.

Fig. 10–1 Celtic Rose, 7" motif. A traditional mandala design that reflects the English heritage of many of America's early settlers.

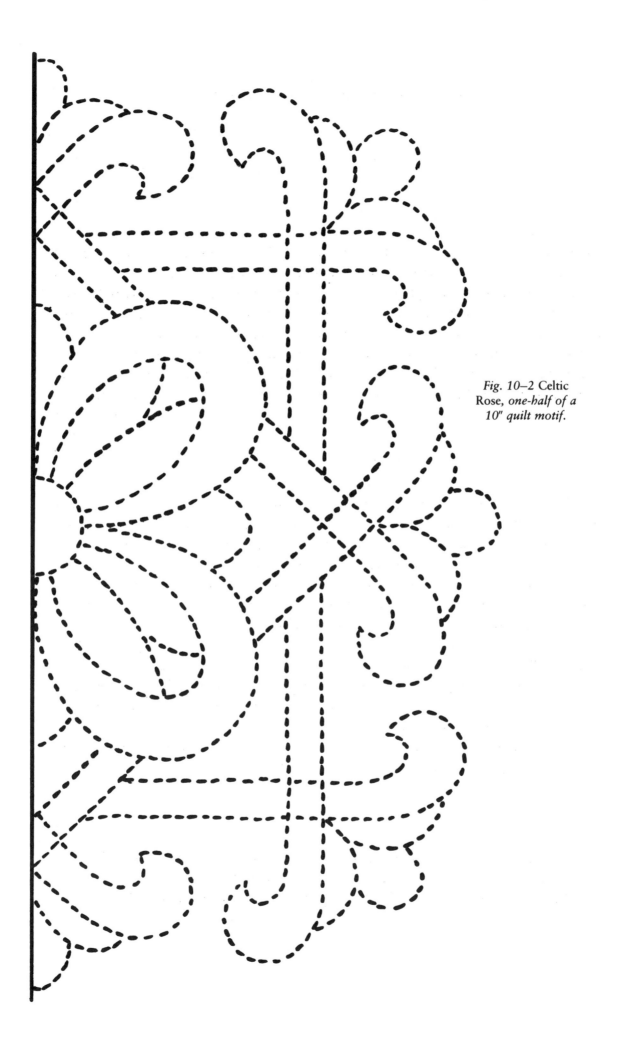

Fig. 10–2 Celtic Rose, one-half of a 10" quilt motif.

Fig. 10–3 Celtic Rose, (a) center area as 5″ block motif; (b) border repeat, 2½″ by 6″.

a

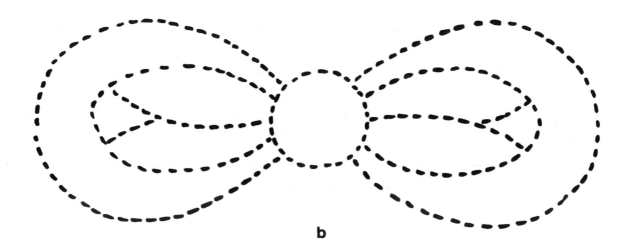

b

Fig. 10–4 Feather and Floral, *6" motif. A quilt motif with a distinctly romantic influence. The feathers are a contemporary version of the traditional feather quilting motifs.*

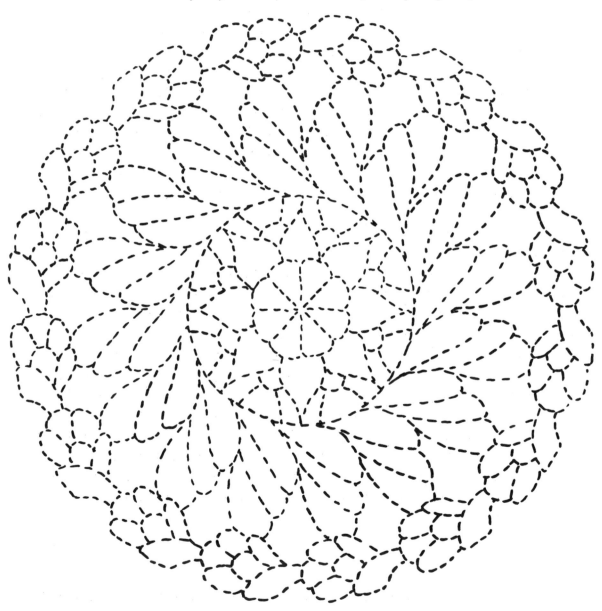

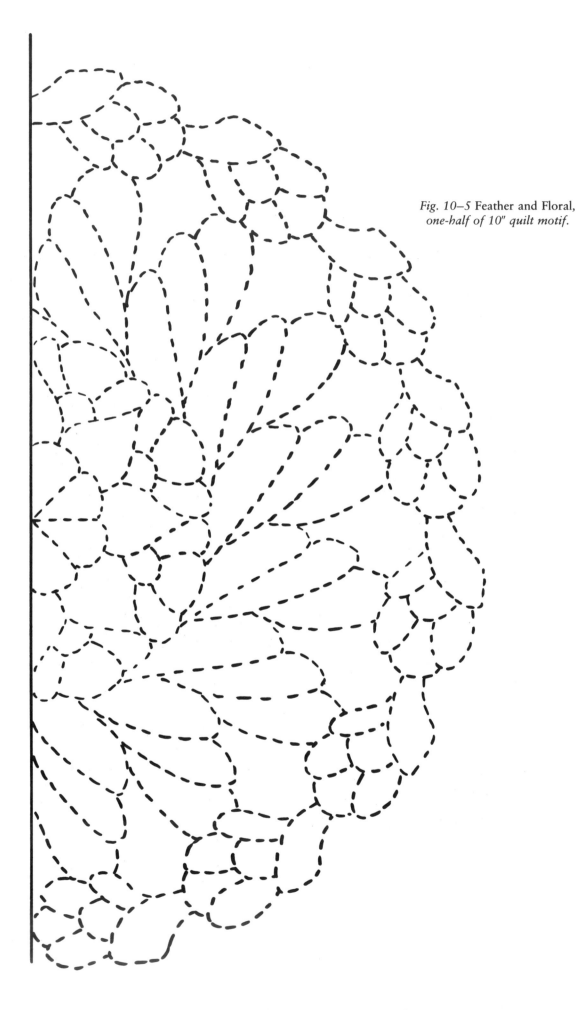

Fig. 10–5 Feather and Floral, one-half of 10" quilt motif.

84

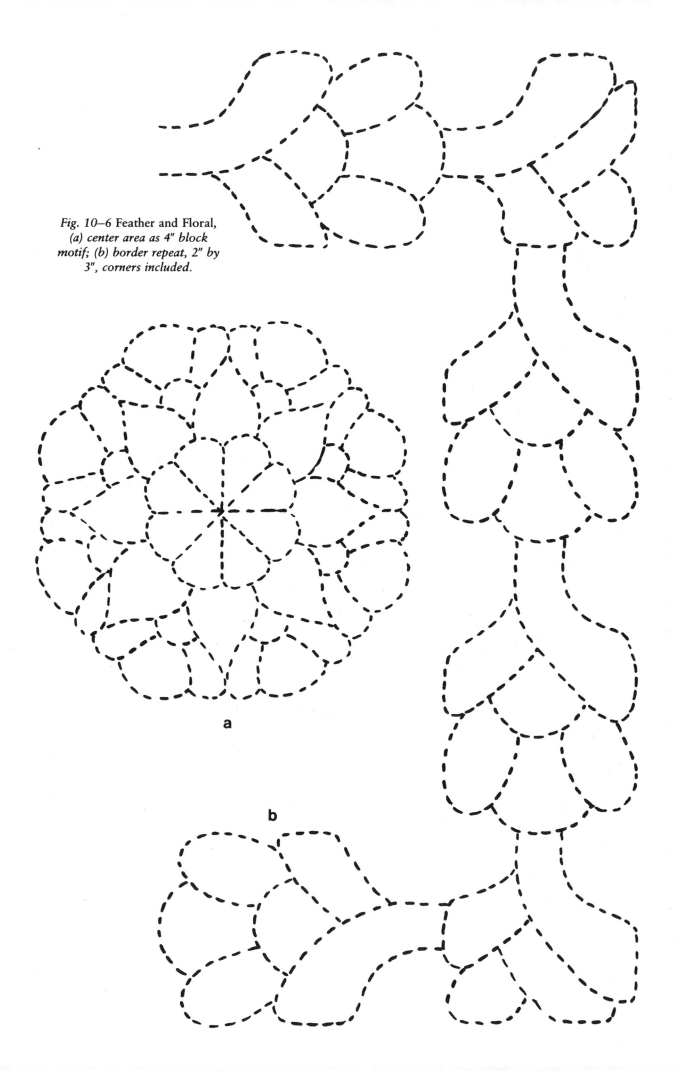

Fig. 10–6 Feather and Floral, (a) center area as 4" block motif; (b) border repeat, 2" by 3", corners included.

a

b

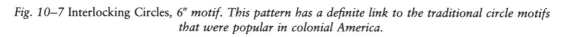

Fig. 10–7 Interlocking Circles, *6" motif. This pattern has a definite link to the traditional circle motifs that were popular in colonial America.*

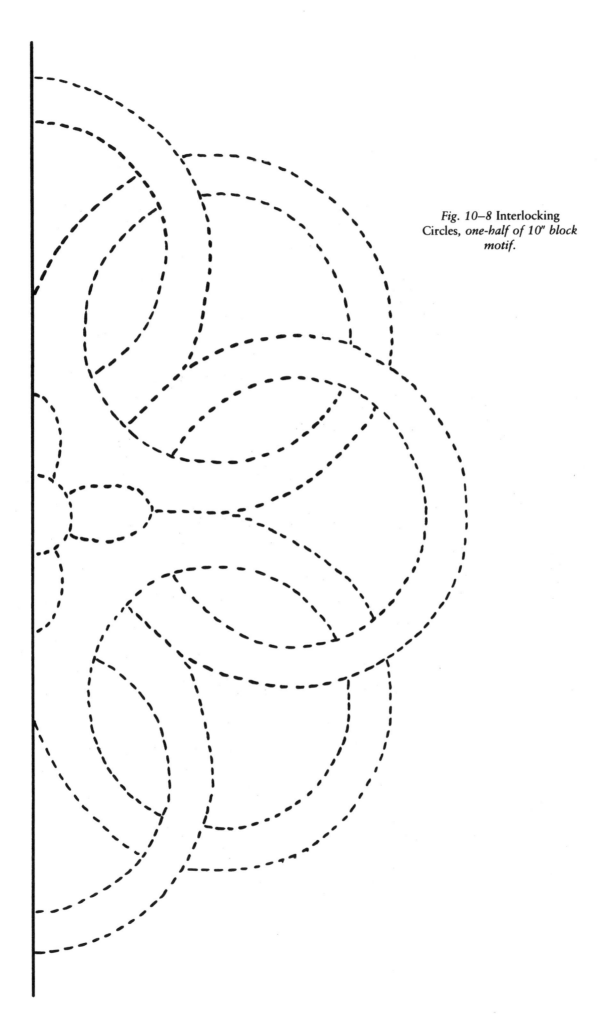

Fig. 10–8 Interlocking Circles, *one-half of 10″ block motif.*

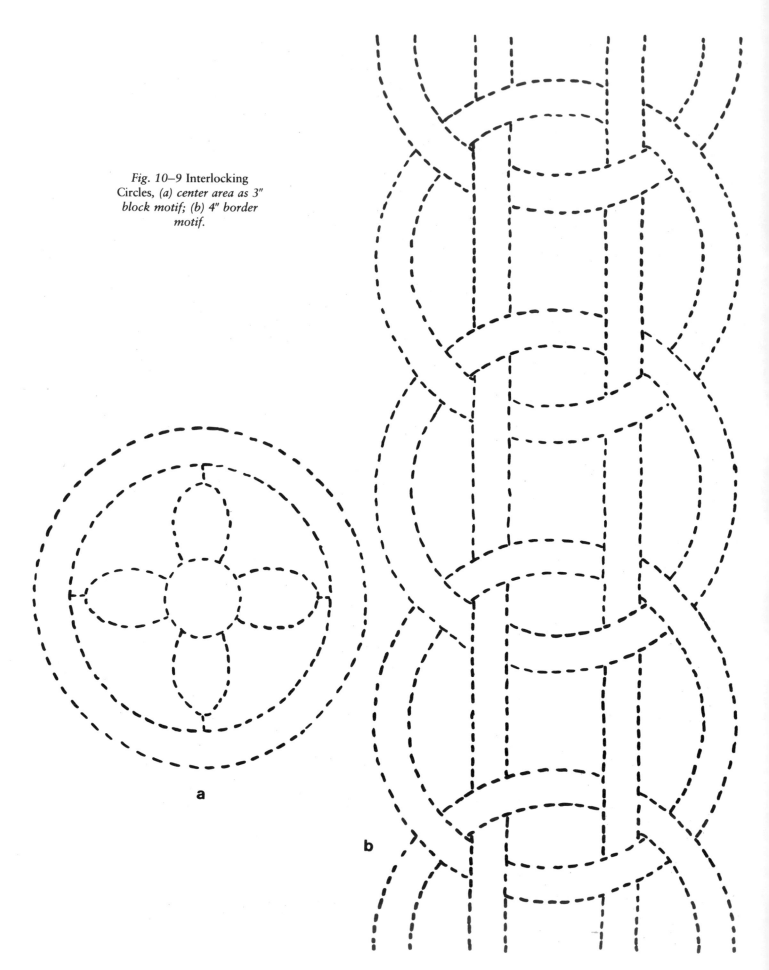

Fig. 10–9 Interlocking Circles, *(a) center area as 3″ block motif; (b) 4″ border motif.*

a

b

Fig. 10–10 Papillon, 7" motif. A contemporary mandala that uses traditional feather quilting on the wings of the butterflies.

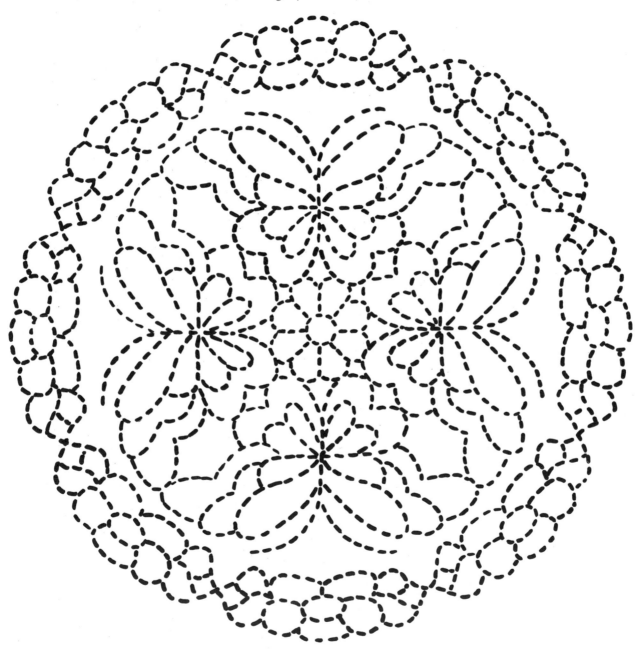

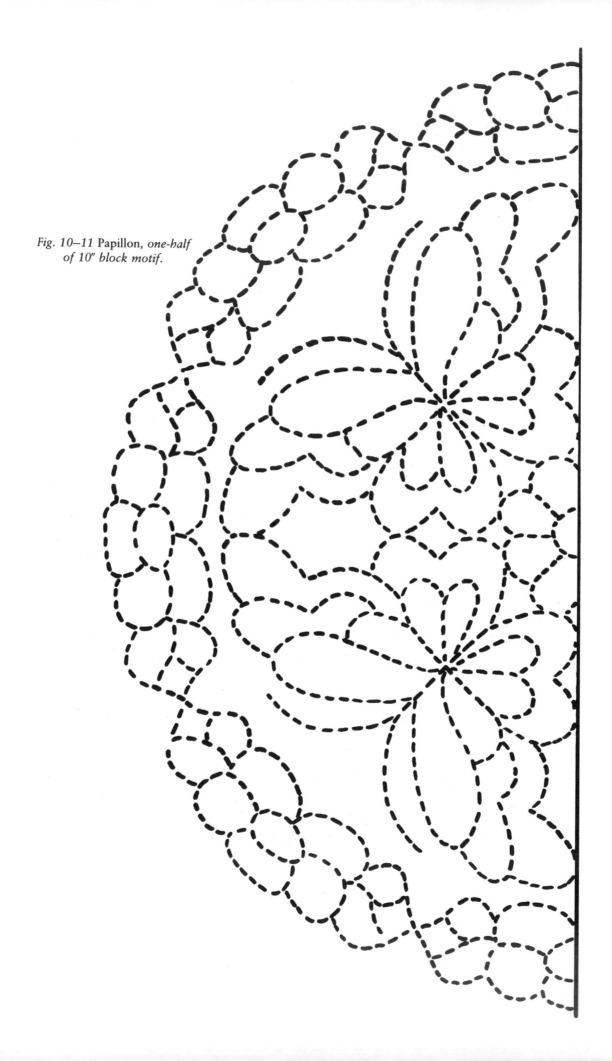

Fig. 10–11 Papillon, *one-half of 10" block motif.*

90

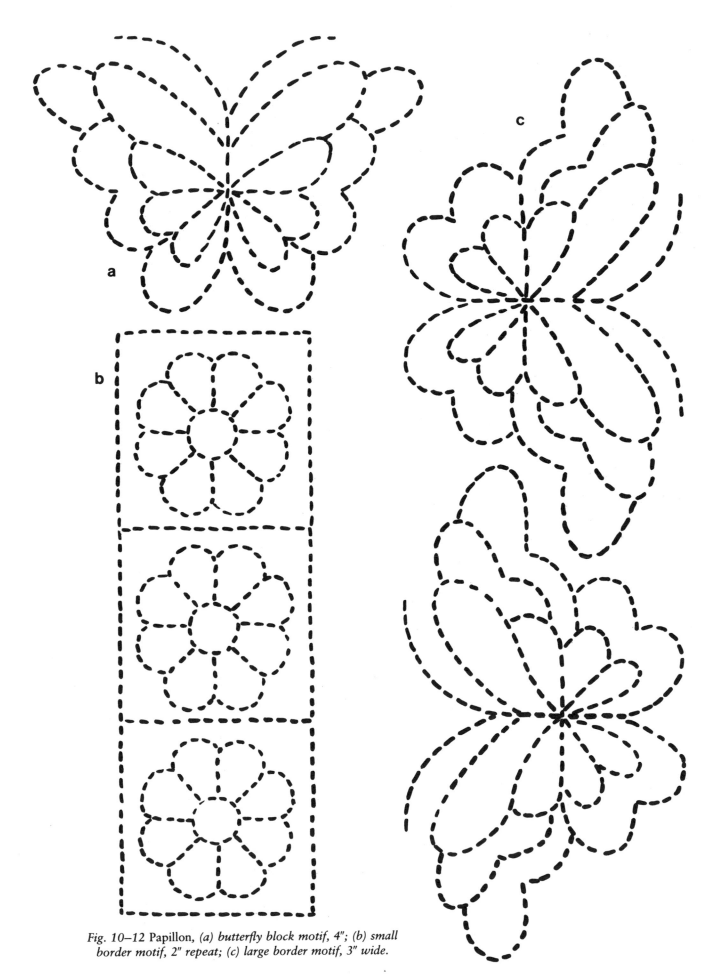

Fig. 10–12 Papillon, (a) butterfly block motif, 4"; (b) small border motif, 2" repeat; (c) large border motif, 3" wide.

91

Fig. 10–13 Scallop Shells, 6″ motif. This motif would be an excellent choice for the center of an "Ocean Waves" block.

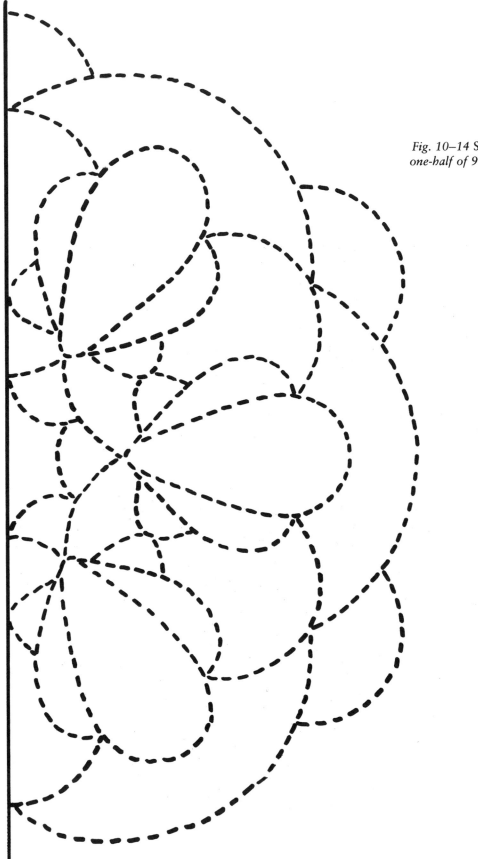

Fig. 10–14 Scallop Shells, *one-half of 9" block motif.*

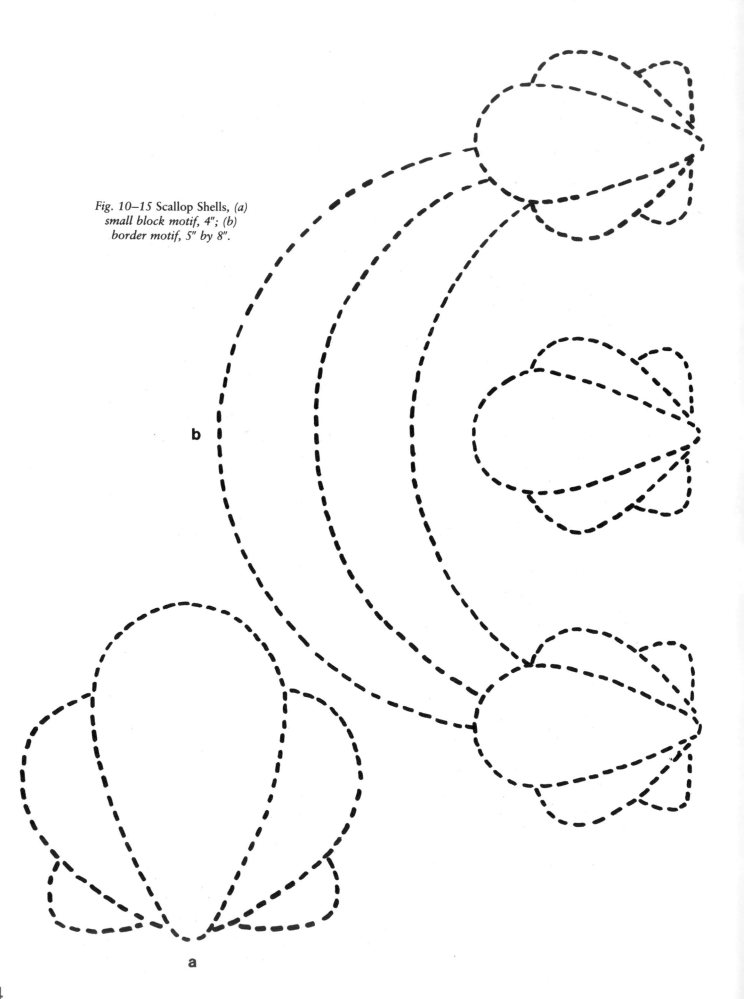

Fig. 10–15 Scallop Shells, (a) small block motif, 4"; (b) border motif, 5" by 8".

b

a

Fig. 10–16 Sunburst, a perfect quilt motif for a 7" block. This design was frequently used as ornamentation on Victorian houses.

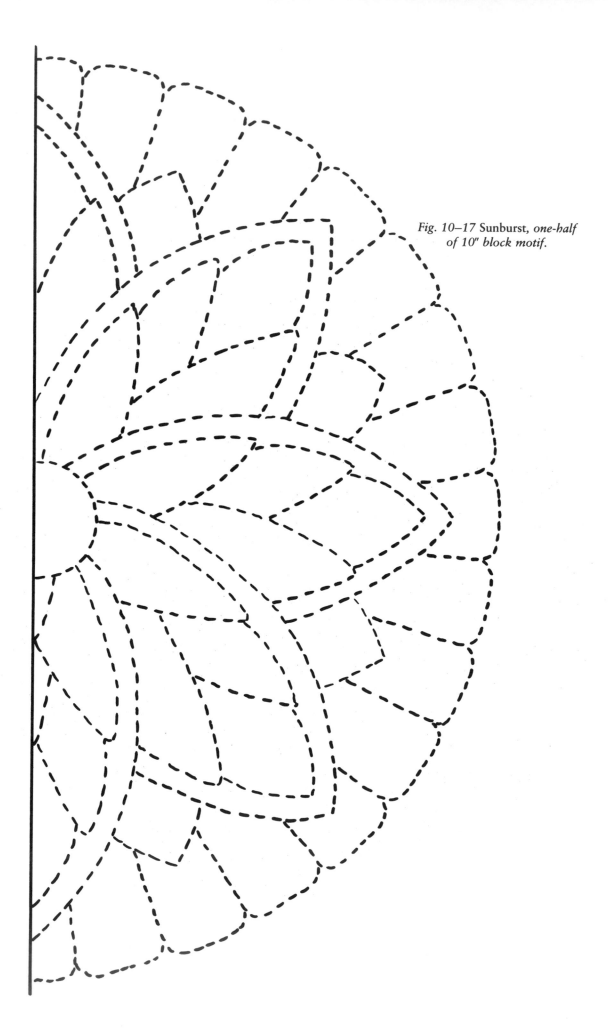

Fig. 10–17 Sunburst, *one-half of 10" block motif.*

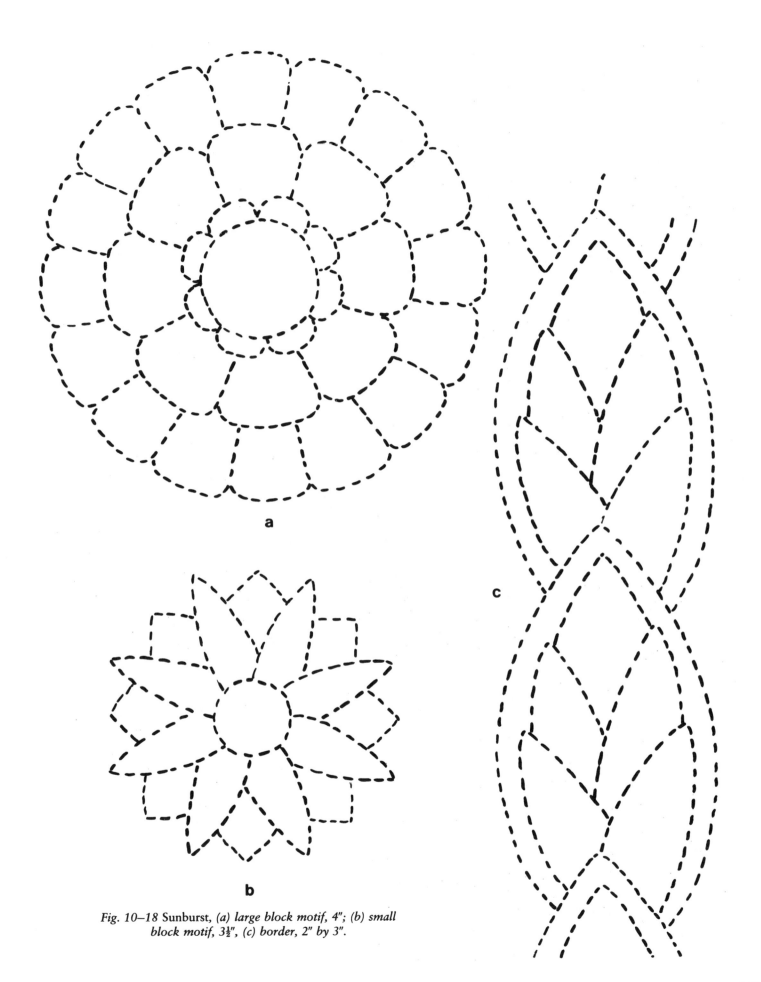

a

b

Fig. 10–18 Sunburst, *(a) large block motif, 4"; (b) small block motif, 3½", (c) border, 2" by 3".*

c

97

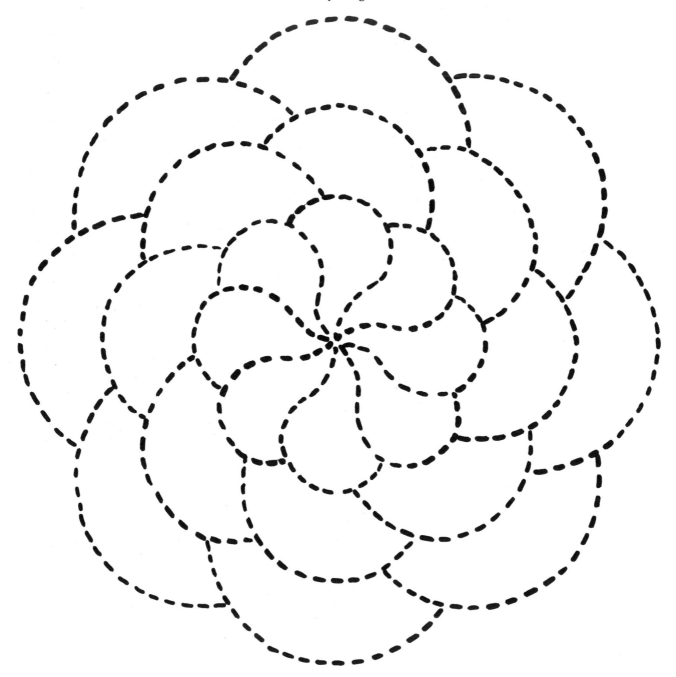

Fig. 10–19 Swirling Scallops, 7" block motif. *A contemporary quilting motif based on traditional scallop designs.*

*Fig. 10–20 Swirling Scallops,
one half of 10″ block motif.*

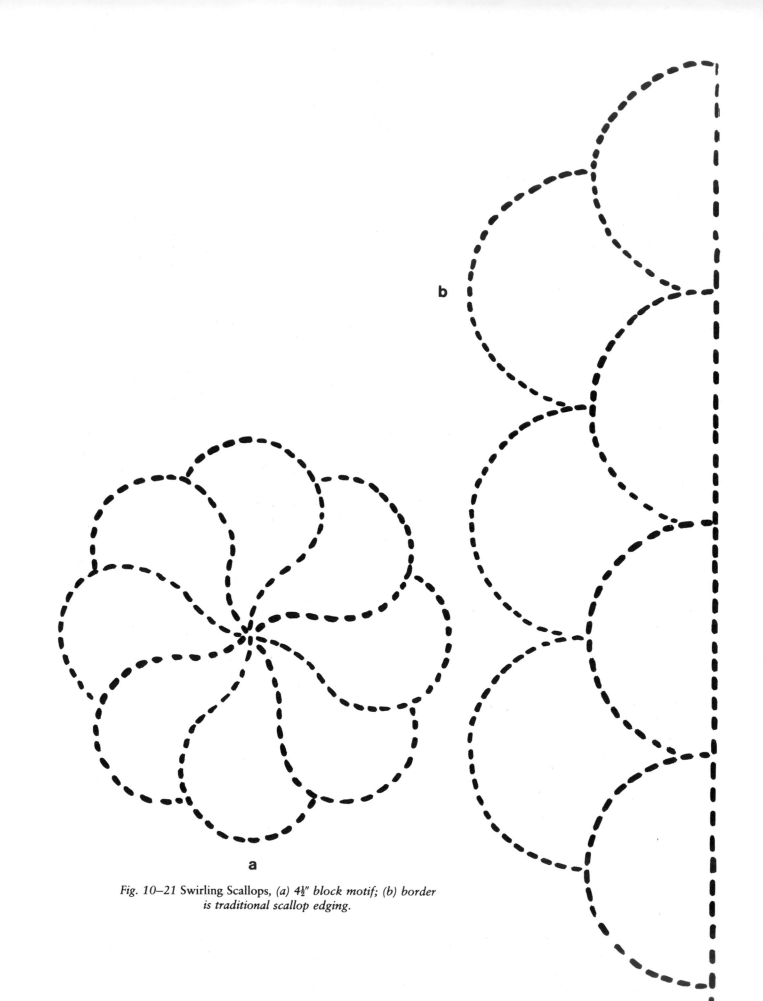

Fig. 10–21 Swirling Scallops, (a) 4½″ block motif; (b) border is traditional scallop edging.

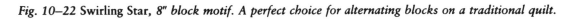
Fig. 10–22 Swirling Star, 8″ block motif. A perfect choice for alternating blocks on a traditional quilt.

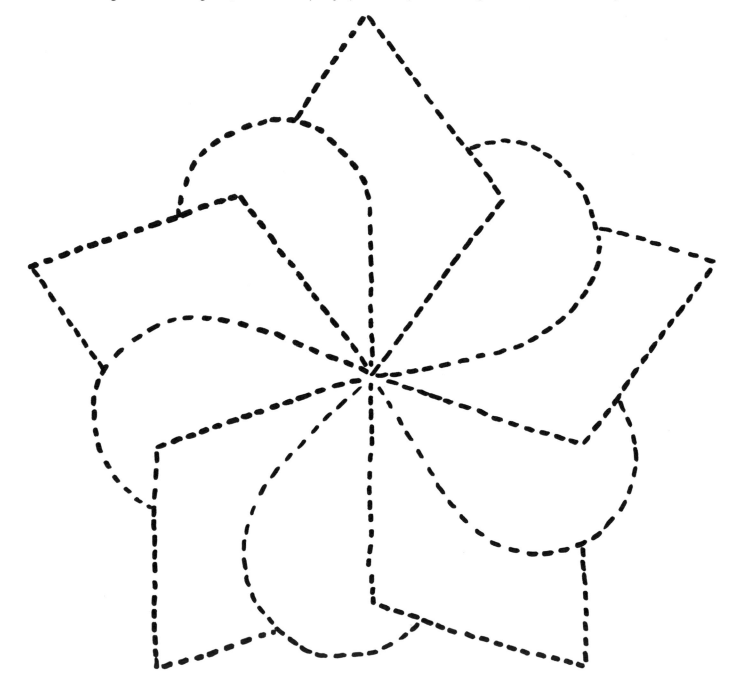

Fig. 10–23 Rose Bouquet, 6" motif. A large single rose in full bloom makes the perfect center for the eight buds in a bridal bouquet motif.

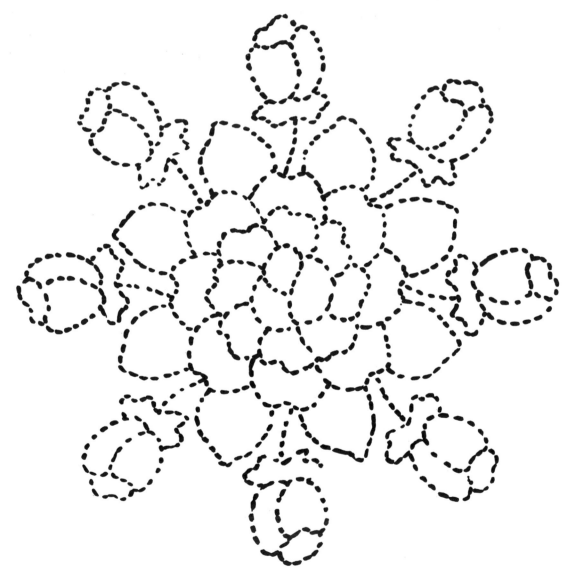

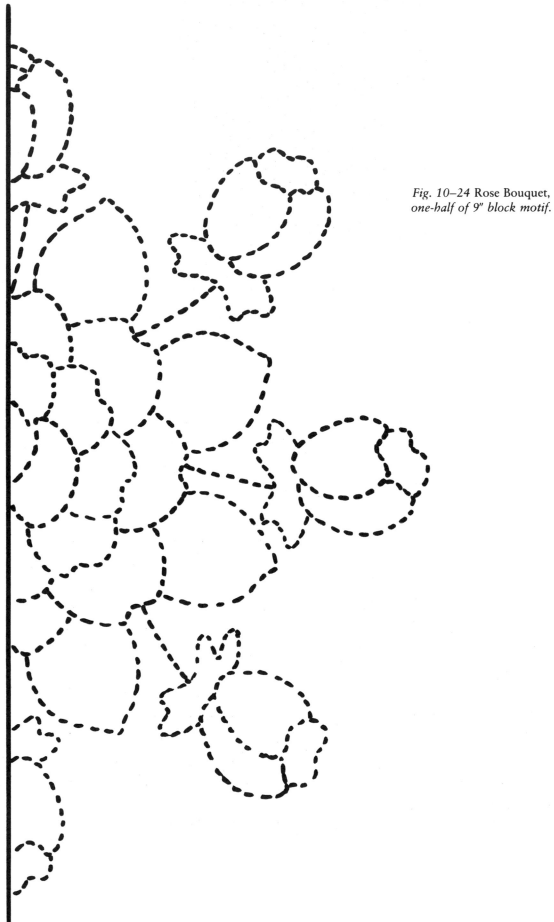

Fig. 10–24 Rose Bouquet, one-half of 9" block motif.

Fig. 10–25 Feathered Hearts, 6" block motif. Hearts and feathers were popular quilting motifs in the past, and here is a new arrangement that is easy to stitch.

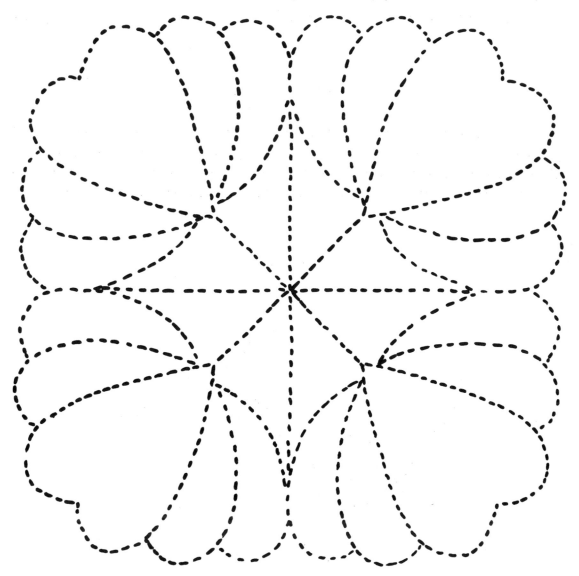

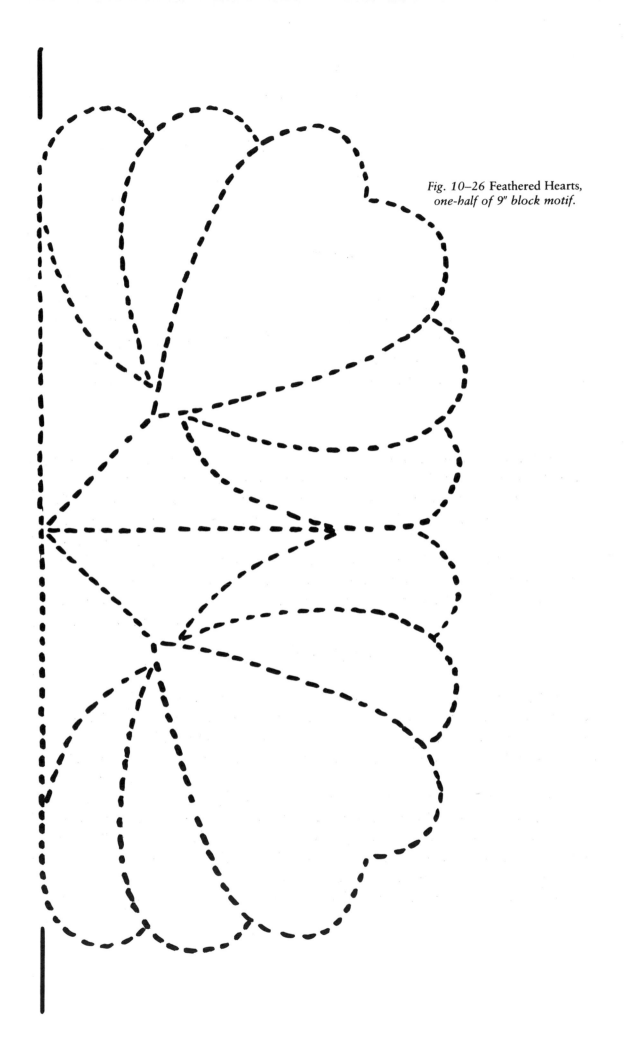

Fig. 10–26 Feathered Hearts, one-half of 9" block motif.

105

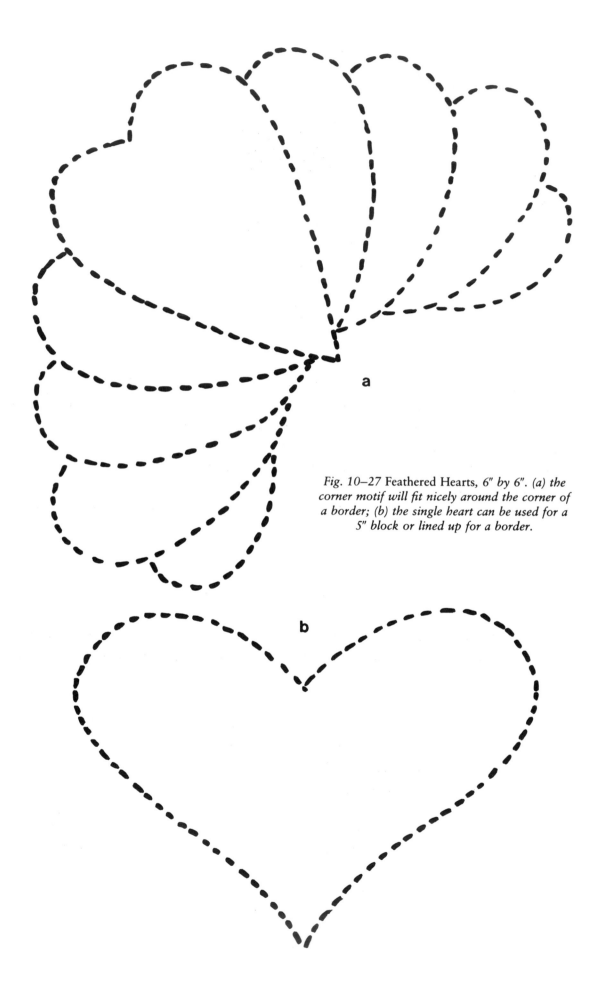

Fig. 10–27 Feathered Hearts, 6" by 6". (a) the corner motif will fit nicely around the corner of a border; (b) the single heart can be used for a 5" block or lined up for a border.

Fig. 10–28 Hearts and Old Lace, 7" block motif. A romantic choice for a bridal quilt or pillow.

Fig. 10–29 Hearts and Old Lace, one-half of 10" block motif.

108

Fig. 10–30 Heart Bouquet, 8" block motif. A simple arrangement that would be a good choice for a traditional quilt.

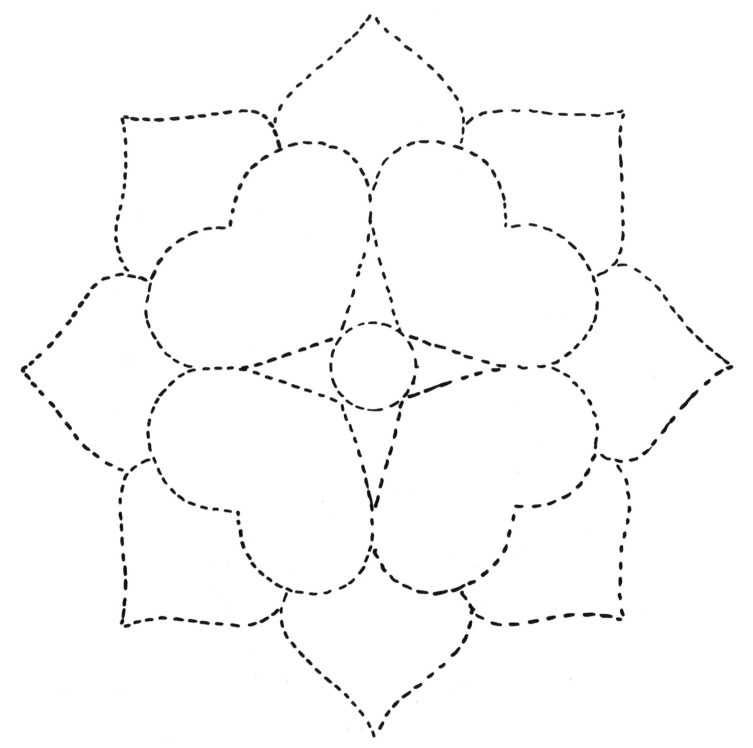

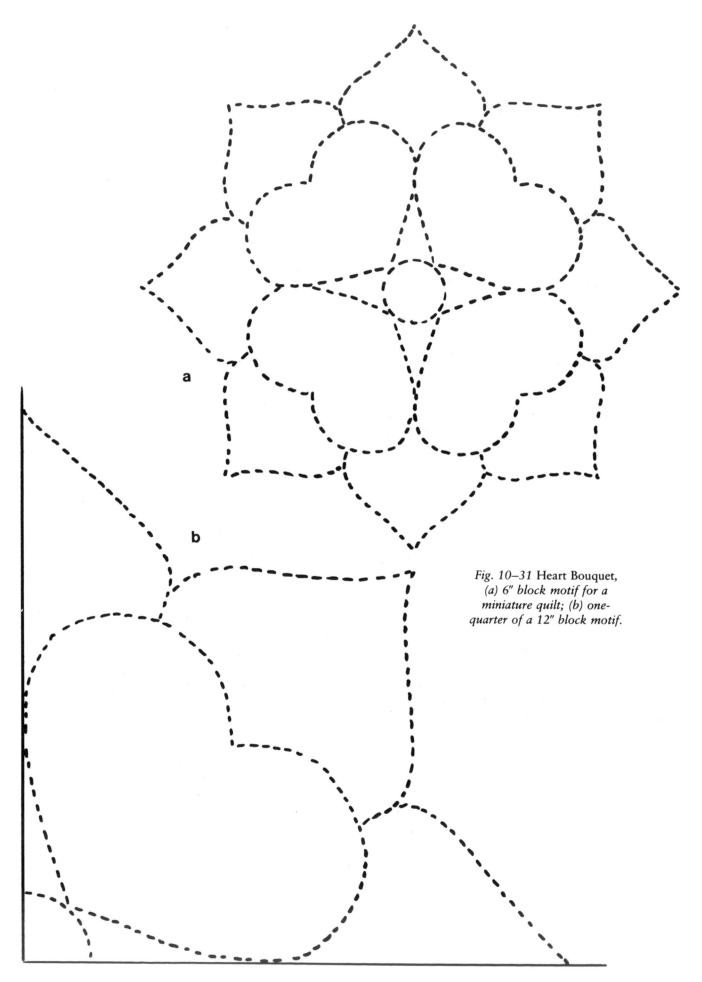

a

b

*Fig. 10–31 Heart Bouquet,
(a) 6" block motif for a
miniature quilt; (b) one-
quarter of a 12" block motif.*

METHODS
AND
MATERIALS

Piecework and appliqué require basic skills that all quiltmakers should acquire whether they consider themselves artists or craftswomen. Contemporary quilt artists should strive not only to create original designs but also to achieve a high standard of craftsmanship. Adequate space in a pleasant environment will provide a good atmosphere for creative activity. Try to set aside some time to work each day. Set small goals for yourself and work toward them, and never allow the volume of work that must go into each individual quilt overwhelm you or inhibit your willingness to begin a project.

– QUILTING SUPPLIES –

Investment in good basic quilting equipment is a must. For accurate pattern drafting and sewing, you will find that you use some basic tools over and over again.

Pattern Drafting Supplies

1. A good metal ruler
2. Pencils and sharpener
3. Graph paper
4. Colored pencils
5. Utility scissors
6. Template materials
7. A right triangle or L-square
8. A protractor
9. A good-quality screw-type compass
10. Masking tape

Sewing Supplies

1. *Thread*
2. *Beeswax*
3. *Sewing needles*
4. *Quilting betweens (sizes 9, 10, and 12)*
5. *Fabric scissors*
6. *Thimbles*
7. *Quilting pins*
8. *Tape measure*
9. *Steam iron*
10. *Large floor frame and round or oval embroidery hoops*

– FABRIC –

Select your quilting fabrics carefully. Closely woven cottons usually have the most body and therefore are the easiest to work with. Remember that you must quilt through three layers, so avoid heavy fabrics such as wools, velvets, denim, or corduroy. Wash and iron all fabrics before cutting them to remove sizing and to prevent shrinking in the finished quilt.

If you select patterned fabrics, carefully consider how you will place them on the quilt top. Use solid fabrics in any areas where you plan to do a quantity of creative hand-quilting. Choose fabrics in light, medium, and dark values to give added dimension to the quilt top.

– TEMPLATES –

Templates for pattern pieces must be accurate if all the pieces are to fit together. Even a small error in size can make a difference when you must cut the same piece over and over for a large quilt top. The easiest way to draw patterns is to use graph paper. The patterns can then be cut out and taped to the template material before you cut the templates.

If you are hand-sewing your quilt, cut geometric shapes to their actual size. Trace around the shape on the wrong side of the fabric. Add a $\frac{1}{4}$-inch seam allowance and cut each piece carefully. For machine piecing, add the $\frac{1}{4}$-inch seam allowance to the template. Trace around the outside of the template on the wrong side of the fabric. You can add extra layers and cut several pieces at once. Use the presser foot of your sewing machine to make sure that the seam allowance remains accurate as your stitch.

For appliqué, prepare the templates in the same method as for piecework. Then trace around the template on the right side of the fabric and add a ¼-inch seam allowance before cutting. The traced pencil line will be your stitching line. As you fasten the pieces in place, tuck the raw edge under along the pencil line using fine pins. Not all edges need to be turned under; some can be tucked under the edge of an adjacent appliqué piece. Wax the thread to strenghthen it and prevent it from tangling.

– APPIQUÉ STITCHES –

You can use one of two methods to secure the fabric—the blind-hem stitch or the overcast stitch (Figure 11–1). Appliquéing on a sewing machine is not recommended if you are making a masterpiece quilt or a quilt for competition. Machine appliqué is appropriate only on baby quilts or in small, decorative hoop pictures, since the stitches will be visible.

Fig. 11–1 Appliqué pieces are pinned in place and ready for (a) blind hem stitching or (b) overcast stitching.

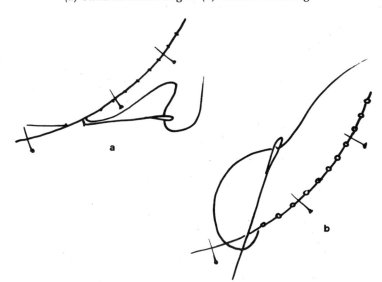

Fig. 11–2 Bars assembled and ready to be sewn as a quilt block.

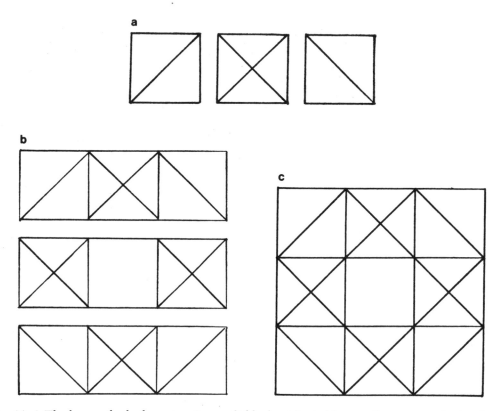

Fig. 11–3 The bar method of constructing quilt blocks: (a) stitching small squares and triangles into larger, square units; (b) joining the square units to make three "bars" of a quilt block; and (c) joining the bars together to make the completed quilt block.

– CONSTRUCTING THE QUILT BLOCKS –

Before you begin sewing, lay all of the pieces of your block out before you to make sure you have cut the right number of pieces. You may also want to change some colors or fabrics at this point, so it is best to begin by cutting one block at a time. Experienced quiltmakers use the bar method of construction (Figures 11–2 and 11–3. First sew all triangles or other geometric shapes into small squares. Then assemble the squares into the appropriate number of bars. Finally, join the bars together to make the completed quilt block.

12

PATTERNS AND PROJECTS

The eighteen patterns on the following pages are primarily block patterns for the center areas of a mandala or magic-circle quilt. Patterns for the whole quilt have been deliberately omitted to encourage you to develop your own unique design. The patterns are to inspire you, the individual quilt artist, to experiment with your own ideas in fabric, color, and quilt-setting arrangements. Any of the block patterns can also be used to make a series of quilt blocks with magic-circle motifs for a quilt set in a more conventional arrangement with sashing or alternating blocks.

Of the quilts in the color section, patterns are given for *Dancing Tulips* (Figure 2), *Arbor Vitae* (Figure 7), *Star Paisley* (Figure 8), *Iris* (Figure 15), *Star of Roses* (cover), *Cockscombs and Currants* (Figure 18), *Evening Star* (Figure 19), and *Navajo Princess* (Figure 20).

If this is the first time you have ventured into designing your own quilt, have patience and don't expect your first efforts to be your best. Whenever you come to an impasse in your work, keep in mind that it will only be temporary. Set the work aside and take a walk, have lunch with a friend, or engage in some other relaxing activity while you work out your solution. Remember that while you are working toward improving your quiltmaking skills, every quilt does not have to be a masterpiece. In fact, some quilts should be made simply for the enjoyment of family and friends.

– USING THE PATTERNS –

The following instructions on how to use the quilt blocks apply to each design. All of the patterns are full-size.

1. The caption for each block diagram gives the block size. Fabric requirements are not given for the individual blocks. If you are a dedicated quiltmaker, you probably have ample fabric on hand to make the blocks. If you want to make a larger quilt, you will need two to three yards of each fabric. If you need to purchase fabric for a particular small block, approximately half a yard for each block will be more than enough.

2. Trace pattern pieces to template material and cut them out. Trace around templates on the right side of the fabric for appliqué pieces. Trace around templates on the wrong side of the fabric for geometric pieced blocks.

3. Wash and iron all fabrics before cutting.

4. Seam allowances are not included in the pattern pieces. Add a $\frac{1}{4}$-inch seam allowance to each piece of fabric and cut them out.

5. Assemble the block according to the block diagram. Use the bar method of construction for pieced blocks as shown in Figures 11–2 and 11–3 in Chapter 11. For appliqué blocks, cut a background square to the size indicated on the block layout. Allow a $\frac{1}{4}$-inch seam allowance on each side. Fold and press the block in half from side to side and from corner to corner. The crease lines will help you place the appliqué pieces accurately. It is also helpful to trace an outline of the block design on the right side of the background fabric to ensure that your pieces are accurately placed.

6. Stitch the blocks in place.

7. Press the blocks carefully.

Fig. 12–1 Star Paisley, 36" block, feathered star design, based on a nine-patch block. Cut 4 print A, 4 medium B, 4 dark C, 16 dark D, 48 light D, 16 medium E, 16 Dark F, 4 light G, 4 light H, 4 print I, 4 light J, 8 print K, and 4 print L. Stitch together as in block diagram.

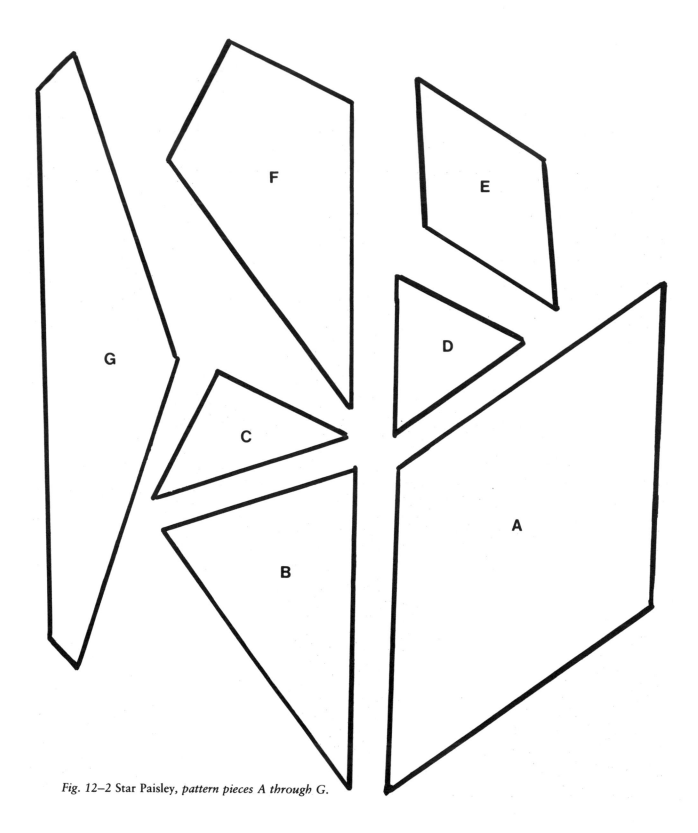

Fig. 12–2 Star Paisley, *pattern pieces A through G.*

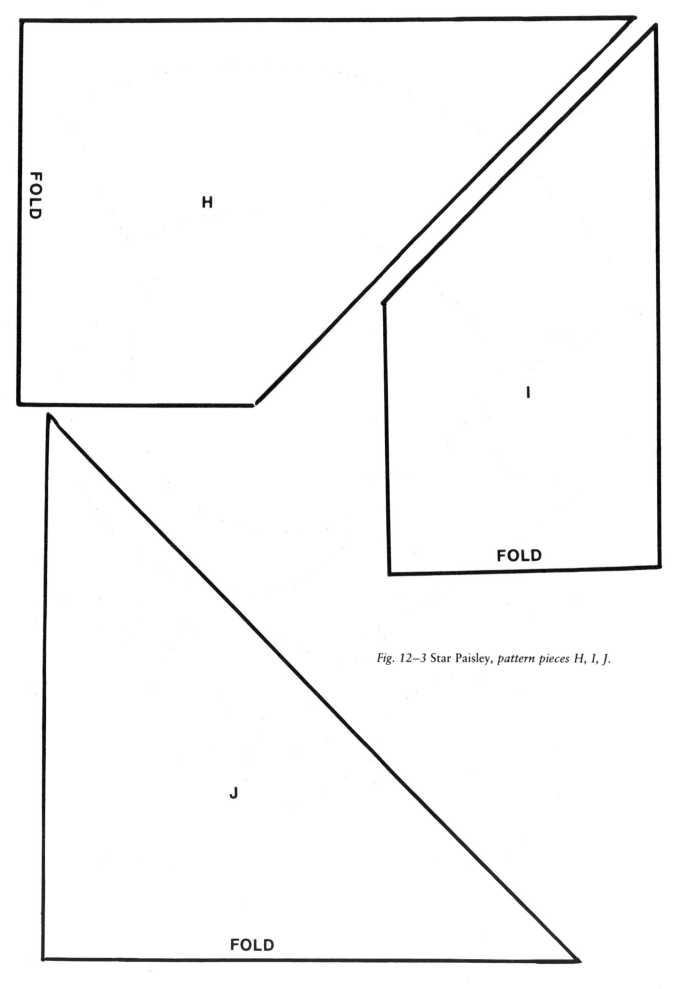

FOLD

H

I

FOLD

Fig. 12–3 Star Paisley, *pattern pieces H, I, J.*

J

FOLD

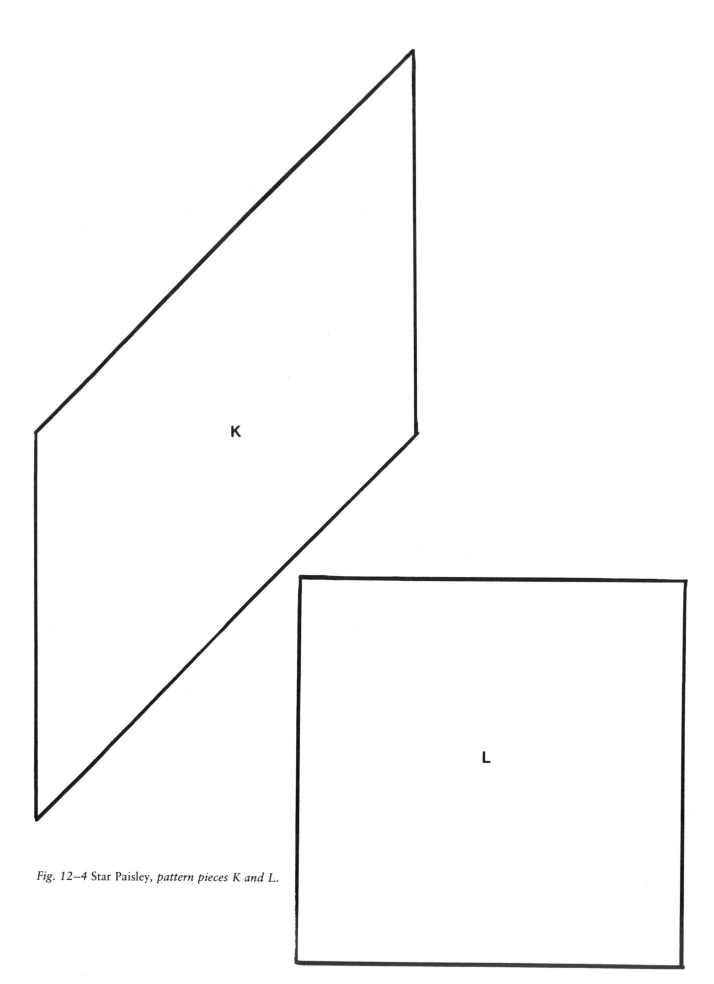

K

L

Fig. 12–4 Star Paisley, *pattern pieces K and L.*

Fig. 12–5 Star of Roses, 14" block, feathered star design. Cut 4 light A, 4 light B, 8 print C, 8 dark D, 32 dark E, 48 light E, 8 dark F, 8 dark G, and 8 print H. Stitch together as in block diagram.

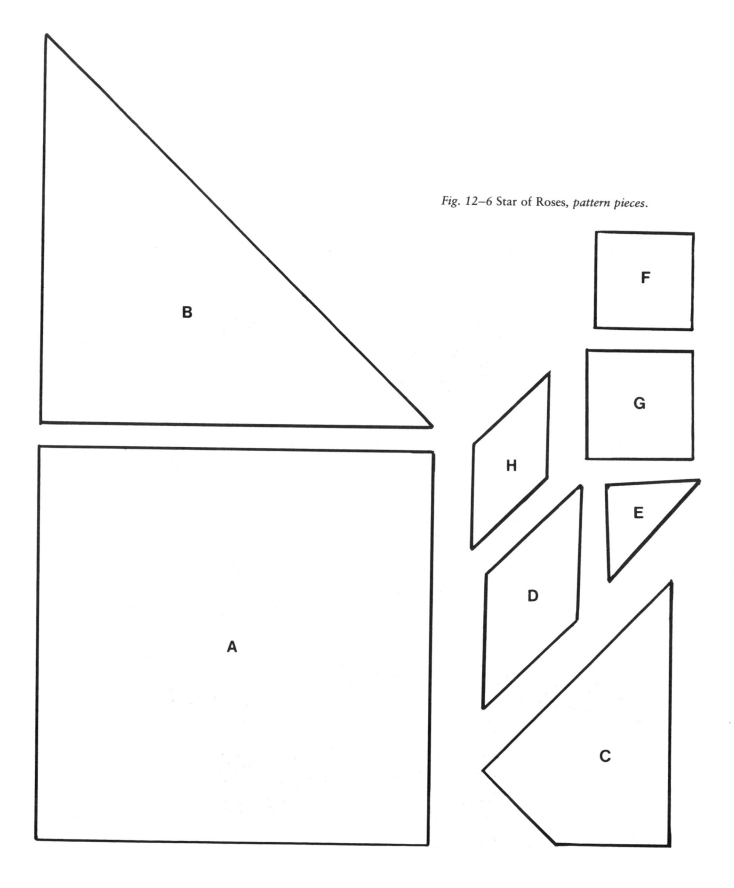

Fig. 12–6 Star of Roses, *pattern pieces.*

Fig. 12–7 Star Flower, 12" block. Cut 1 light A, 4 light B, 8 print C, 4 dark D, 24 dark E, 24 light E, 1 dark F, 4 print G, 4 dark H, and 4 print I. Stitch together as in block diagram.

Fig. 12–8 Star Flower, *pattern pieces*.

126

Fig. 12–9 Syzygy, 10" "Compass" block. Cut 1 dark A, 8 dark B, 8 medium C, 16 light D, 8 medium E, 7 dark F, 1 dark G, and 1 print H on fold. Cut a 27" light square for the appliqué block.

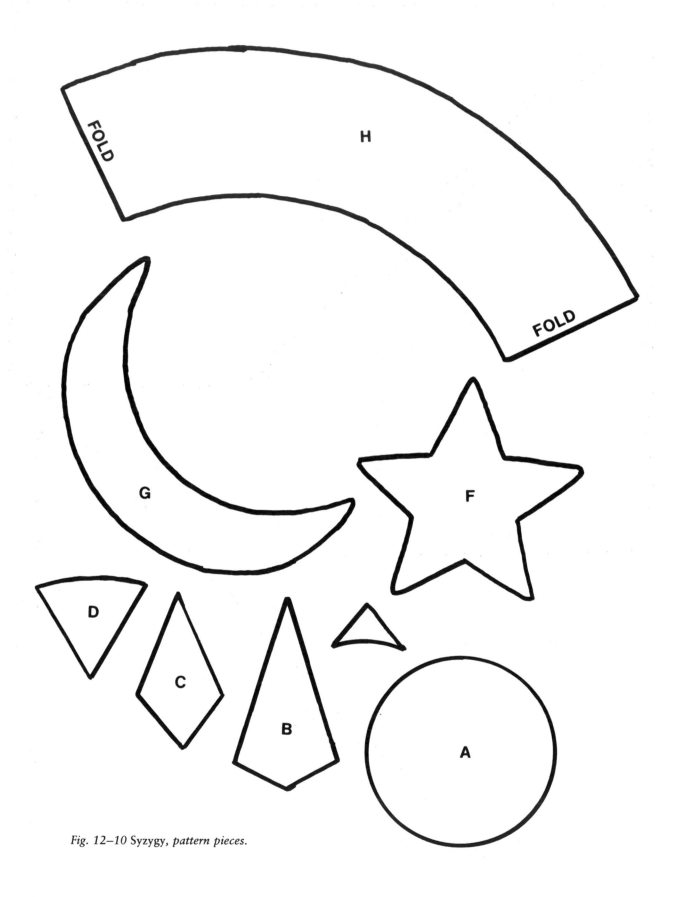

Fig. 12–10 Syzygy, *pattern pieces.*

Fig. 12–11 Evening Star, 10″ block. Cut 1 print A, 4 dark print B, 8 light C, 4 light D, and 4 print E. Stitch together as in block diagram.

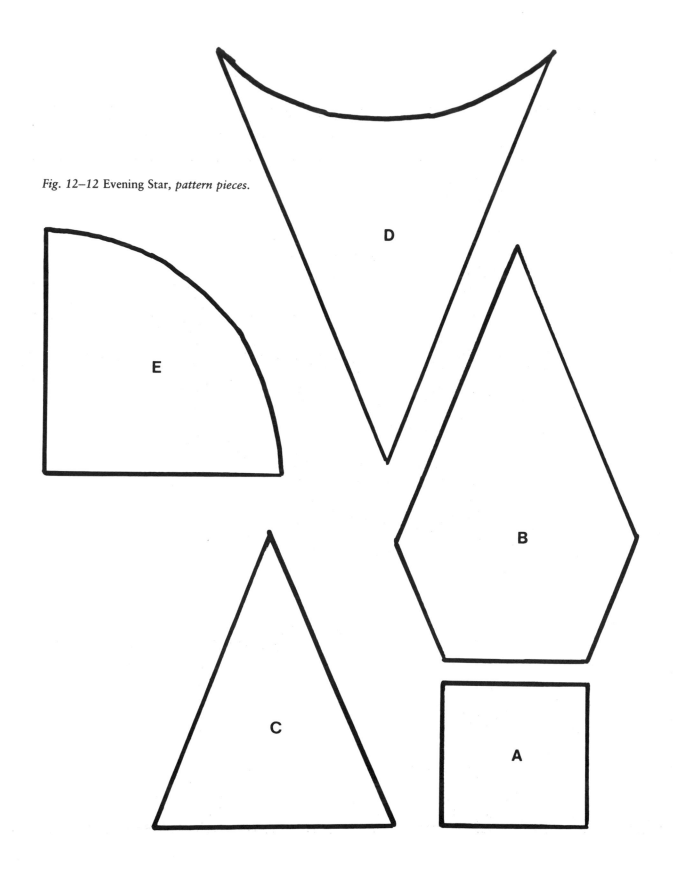

Fig. 12–12 Evening Star, *pattern pieces.*

Fig. 12–13 Morning Star, *10" block. Cut 4 light print A, 16 light B, 16 dark print C, 8 light D, 8 light E, 8 dark print F, and 1 dark print G.*

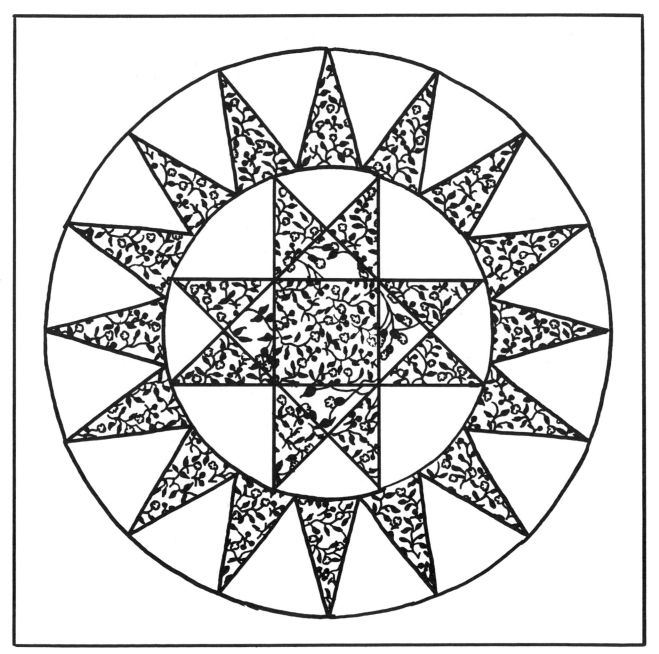

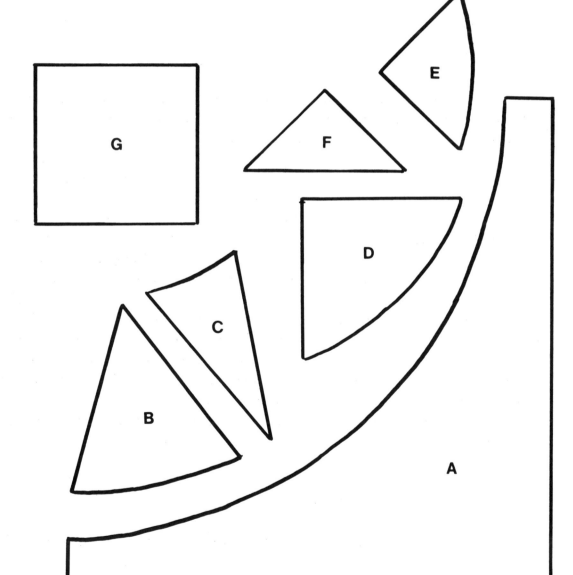

Fig. 12–14 Morning Star, *pattern pieces.*

Fig. 12–15 Arbor Vitae, "Tree of Life," 18" block pattern. Trace pattern pieces and tape together to make full-size appliqué tree pattern. Cut from green fabric. Cut 52 red berries, 8 green vines, and 4 red hearts. Cut 4 corner triangles 18" along base and 9" high at center. Stitch according to block diagram.

Fig. 12–16 Arbor Vitae, *right quadrant.*

Fig. 12–17 Arbor Vitae, *left quadrant.*

Fig. 12–18 Arbor Vitae, *top quadrant.*

Fig. 12–19 Arbor Vitae, *bottom quadrant.*

Fig. 12–20 Arbor Vitae, *heart-and-vine pattern, one-half corner triangle.*

FOLD LINE

Fig. 12–21 Navajo Princess, 36" block. Cut 8 medium A, 8 light B, 8 dark C, 16 medium D, and 8 dark E. Appliqué to background square.

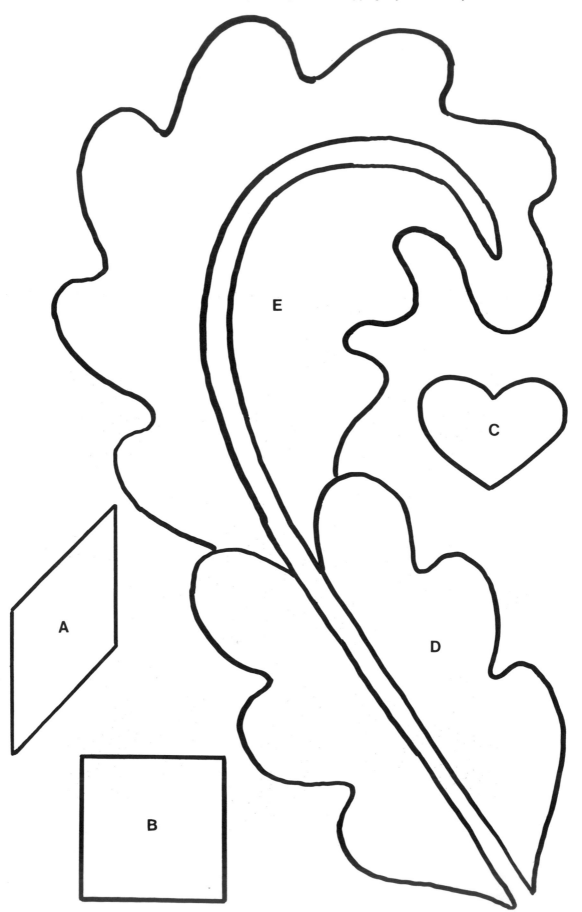

Fig. 12–22 Navajo Princess, *pattern pieces and appliqué placement layout.*

Fig. 12–23 Cockscombs and Currants, 22" block. Cut 1 light A, 1 dark B, 16 dark C, 20 medium C, 4 dark D, 4 medium E, 4 dark F, 4 medium F, and 4 medium G. Appliqué in place.

Fig 12–24 Cockscombs and Currants, *pattern pieces.*

142

Fig. 12–25 Iris, 14" block. Cut 4 light green A, 4 light green B, 1 yellow C, 4 medium peach D, 4 yellow E, 4 dark peach F, 8 medium peach G, 8 light peach H, and 4 green I. Appliqué in place.

Fig. 12–26 Iris, one-quarter block diagram. Trace for pattern layout.

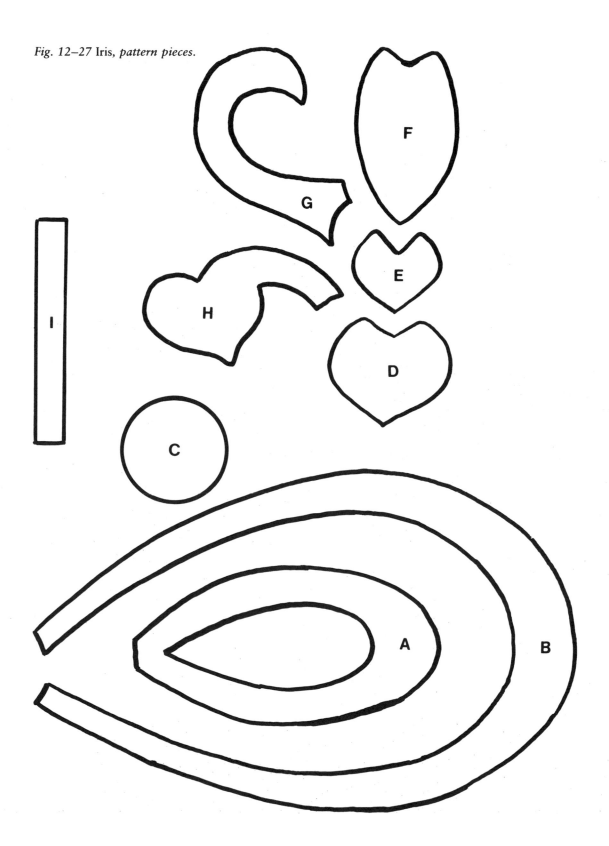

Fig. 12–27 Iris, *pattern pieces.*

Fig. 12–28 Tulip Hearts, *14" block. Cut 4 light A, 4 medium B, 1 dark C, 4 medium D, and 4 light E.*
Cut 4 pieces of bias for the stems, 1" by 3". Appliqué in place.

Fig. 12–29 Tulip Hearts, *one-quarter block diagram for pattern layout.*

Fig. 12–30 Tulip Hearts, *pattern pieces.*

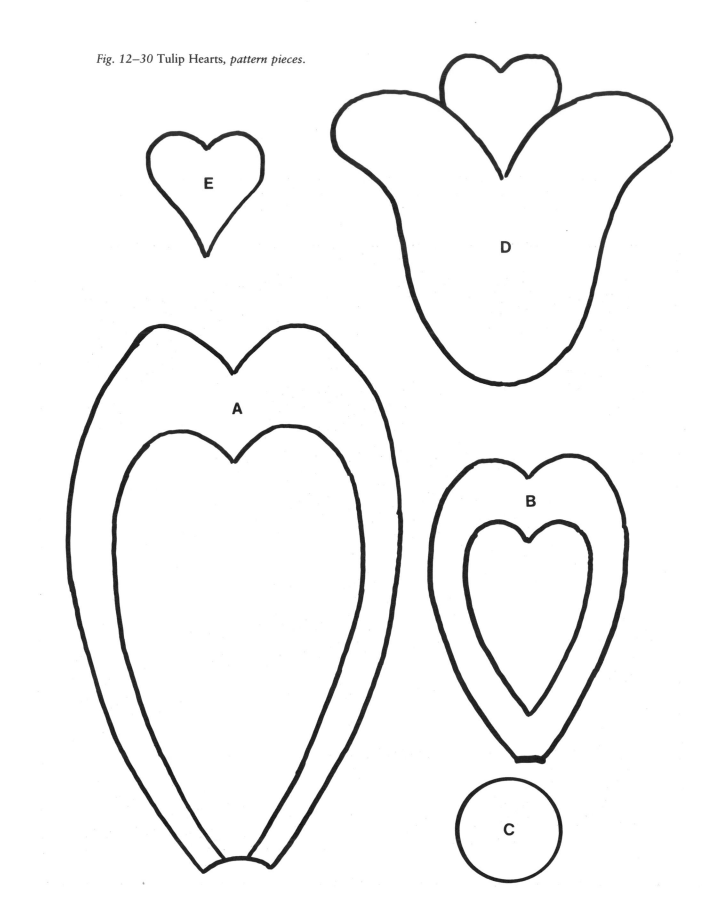

Fig. 12–31 Circle of Hearts, 14" block. Cut 1 dark A, 4 dark B, 4 green C, 4 dark print D, 20 print E, and 4 dark print F. Appliqué in place.

Fig 12–32 Circle of Hearts, *one-quarter block diagram.*

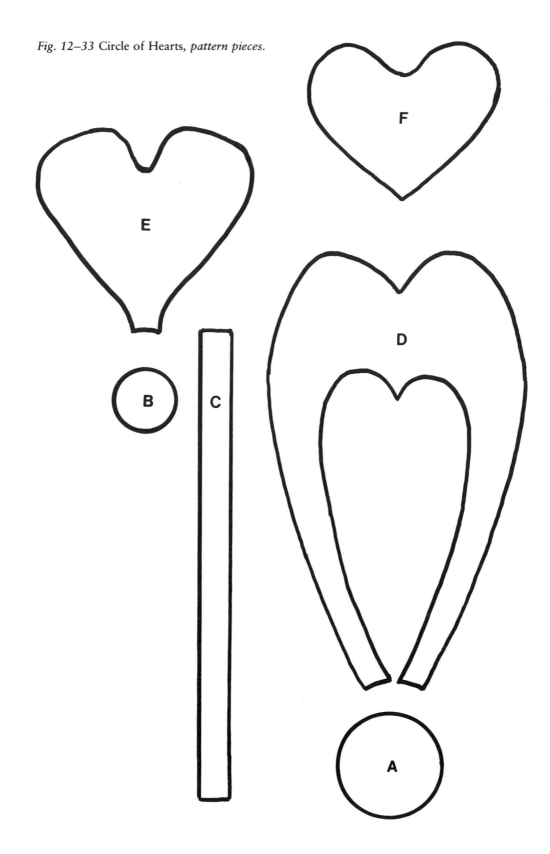

Fig. 12–33 Circle of Hearts, *pattern pieces.*

Fig. 12–34 Sweetheart Roses, 12″ block. Cut 1 light A, 1 green B, 12 dark C, 6 medium D, 6 light E, 6 light F, and 6 green G. Appliqué in place.

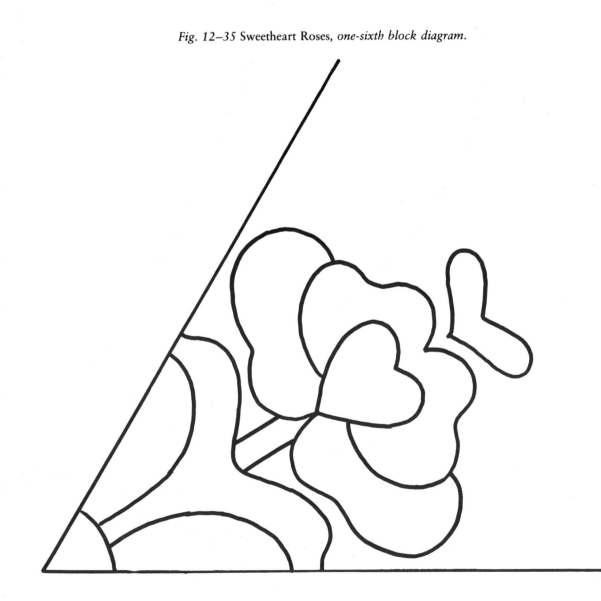

Fig. 12–35 Sweetheart Roses, *one-sixth block diagram.*

Fig. 12–36 Sweetheart Roses, *pattern pieces.*

154

Fig. 12–37 Wood Lily, 12" block. Trace both halves of block on paper to make full-size block. Cut 6 green leaves—half of each leaf dark green, half of each leaf medium green. Cut 3 full petals from medium peach, pink, or yellow. Cut 3 half petals from dark peach, pink, or yellow. Appliqué in place. Embroider stamens with floss.

155

Fig. 12–38 Wood Lily, *left half of full-size block.*

FIg. 12–39 Wood Lily, *right half of full-size block.*

Fig. 12–40 Dancing Tulips, 25" block. Cut 1 dark A, 4 dark print B, 8 green C, 8 dark print D, 16 green E, and 16 dark F. Appliqué in place. OPTION: *Using black bias, stitch over outline edges of appliqué pieces for a stained-glass effect.*

Fig. 12–41 Dancing Tulips, *pattern pieces.*

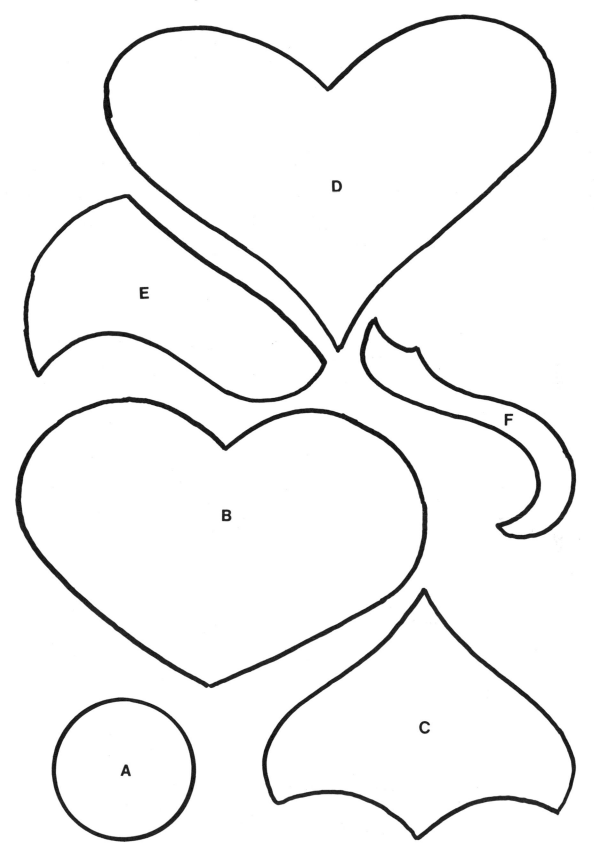

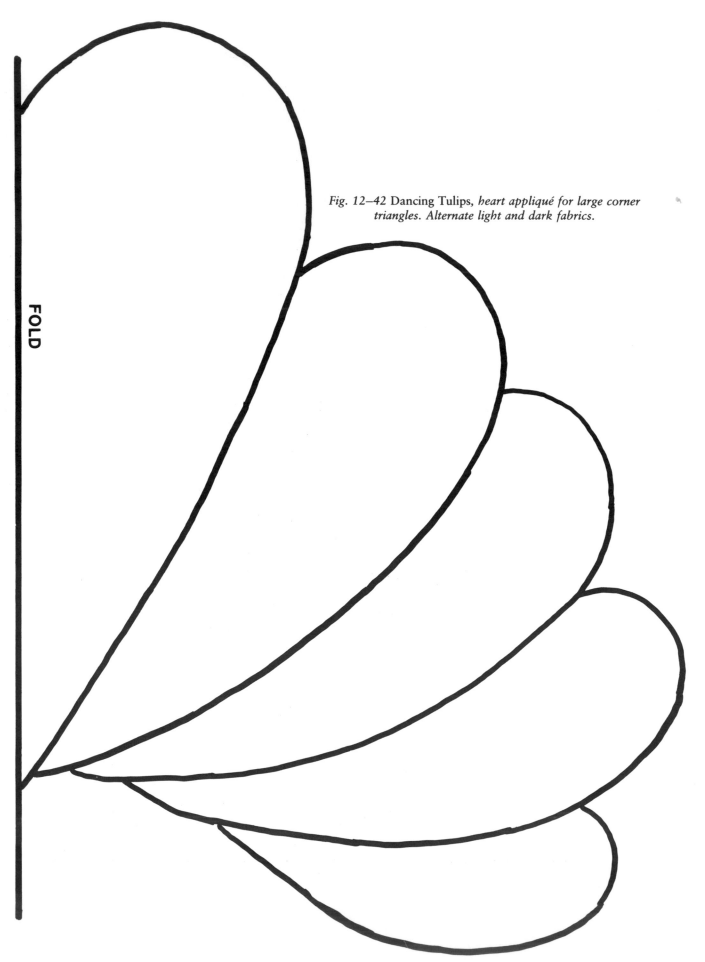

FOLD

Fig. 12–42 Dancing Tulips, heart appliqué for large corner triangles. Alternate light and dark fabrics.

Fig. 12–43 Orchid Ballet, 25" block. Cut 1 dark A, 8 medium green B, 8 dark green C, 8 light green D, 24 dark E, 8 each medium F, G, H, I, and J, 8 dark K, 8 light L, 8 medium M, and 8 yellow N.

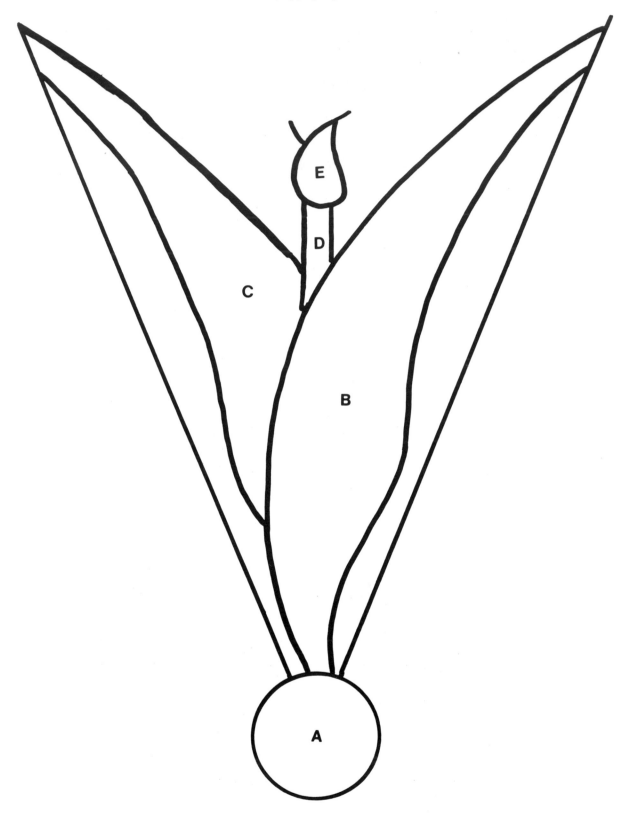

Fig. 12–44 Orchid Ballet, *appliqué patterns and center half; one-eighth block diagram for placement of appliqué pieces.*

Fig. 12–45 Orchid Ballet, *appliqué patterns and top half of one-eighth diagram for placement of appliqué pieces.*

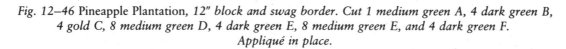

Fig. 12–46 Pineapple Plantation, 12" block and swag border. Cut 1 medium green A, 4 dark green B, 4 gold C, 8 medium green D, 4 dark green E, 8 medium green E, and 4 dark green F. Appliqué in place.

Fig. 12–47 Pineapple Plantation, *one-quarter block diagram.*

Fig. 12—48 Pineapple Plantation, *pattern pieces.*

Fig. 12–49 Pineapple Plantation, *swag border, 6" repeat. Cut pineapple pieces same as block. Cut narrow swag from medium green and wide swag from dark green. Appliqué dark swag first, then appliqué medium swag on top.*

Fig. 12–50 Victorian Rose, 15" block. Cut 1 burgundy A, 1 light-medium pink B, 1 light pink C, 1 medium pink D and E, 8 dark pink varied prints F, 8 light pink varied prints G, 8 dark green H, 8 medium green I, 8 dark green J, 8 medium green K, 8 medium pink L, 8 dark pink M, 8 light pink N, and 8 burgundy O. Trace block onto background fabric and appliqué.

Fig. 12–51 Victorian Rose, block diagram. Trace rose pattern according to marked center. Rotate diagram to mark leaf and bud placement.

169

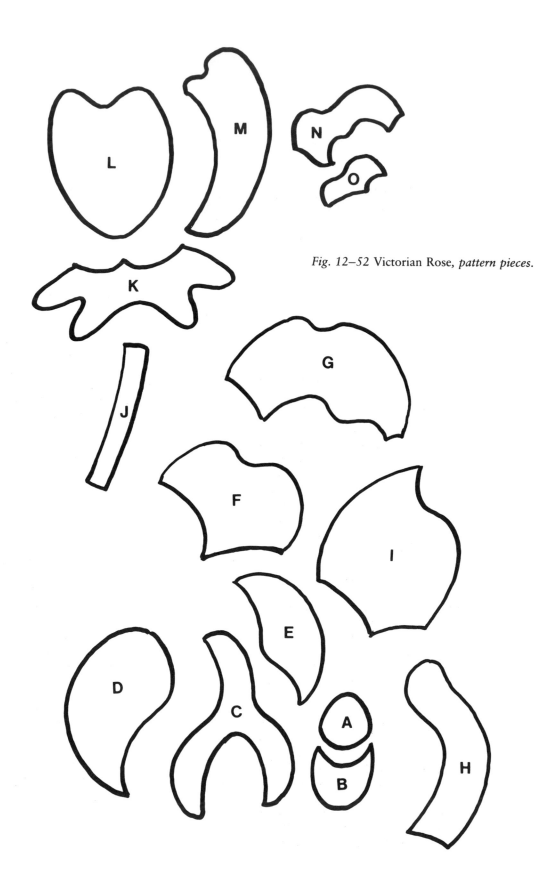

Fig. 12–52 Victorian Rose, *pattern pieces.*

BIBLIOGRAPHY

Arguelles, Jose. *Mandala*. Berkeley, Calif.: Shambala Publications, 1972.

Birren, Faber. *Color Psychology and Color Therapy*. Secaucus, N.J.: The Citadel Press, 1950.

————.*History of Color in Painting*. New York: Van Nostrand Reinhold, 1965.

————.*The Textile Colorist*. New York: Van Nostrand Reinhold, 1980.

Kandinsky, Wassily. *Concerning the Spiritual in Art*. New York: Dover Publications, 1977.

Houck, Carter, ed. *Lady's Circle Patchwork Quilts*. New York: Lopez Publications, 1983.

Houser, Jim. *Color for the Artist*. West Palm Beach, Fla., 1975.

Jung, Carl. *Man and His Symbols*. New York: Doubleday, 1964.

Wright, Janet Izard. *The Mandala Coloring Pad*. New York: Doubleday, 1972.

INDEX

Page numbers in *italics* refer to black-and-white illustrations;
figure numbers refer to color section